THIS BOOK BELONGS TO:

NAME	
ADDRESS	
PHONE #	
EMAIL	

DEDICATION

This Clothing Reseller Inventory Log Book is dedicated to resellers who want to keep accurate records and retain information for your online business.

You are my inspiration for producing this book and I'm honored to be a part of helping you manage and retain important information regarding your resale business.

HOW TO USE THIS BOOK

This Clothing Reseller Inventory Log Book will help you record, collect, and organize your information in an easy to use format.

Here are examples of information for you to fill in and write the details for your activities as a clothing reseller.

Fill in the following information:

1. Listing Tracker - record inventory number, item, brand, description, source of purchase, source location, cost, category (men, women, kids), condition (new with tags, preowned)

2. Details - list material, style, flaws

3. Sizing - record tag size, chest, length, waist, sleeve, neck, shoulder, inseam, and rise

4. Sales Information - record date sold, listing price, sold price, shipping cost, seller fees, total expenses, and profit

5. Notes - space to write extra information

INVENTORY #		ITEM		BRAND	

DESCRIPTION	

SOURCE		LOCATION		COST	

CATEGORY	WOMEN ☐ MEN ☐ KIDS ☐	CONDITION	NEW WITH TAGS ☐ PREOWNED ☐

DETAILS	MATERIAL	
	STYLE	
	FLAWS	

SIZING	TAG SIZE		WAIST		SHOULDER	
	CHEST		SLEEVE		INSEAM	
	LENGTH		NECK		RISE	

DATE SOLD	LISTING PRICE	SOLD PRICE	SHIPPING COST	SELLER FEES	TOTAL EXPENSE	PROFIT

NOTES

INVENTORY #		ITEM		BRAND	

DESCRIPTION	

SOURCE		LOCATION		COST	

CATEGORY	WOMEN ☐ MEN ☐ KIDS ☐	CONDITION	NEW WITH TAGS ☐ PREOWNED ☐

DETAILS	MATERIAL	
	STYLE	
	FLAWS	

SIZING	TAG SIZE		WAIST		SHOULDER	
	CHEST		SLEEVE		INSEAM	
	LENGTH		NECK		RISE	

DATE SOLD	LISTING PRICE	SOLD PRICE	SHIPPING COST	SELLER FEES	TOTAL EXPENSE	PROFIT

NOTES

INVENTORY #			ITEM		BRAND	

DESCRIPTION	

SOURCE		LOCATION		COST	

CATEGORY WOMEN ☐ MEN ☐ KIDS ☐ **CONDITION** NEW WITH TAGS ☐ PREOWNED ☐

DETAILS	MATERIAL	
	STYLE	
	FLAWS	

SIZING	TAG SIZE		WAIST		SHOULDER	
	CHEST		SLEEVE		INSEAM	
	LENGTH		NECK		RISE	

DATE SOLD	LISTING PRICE	SOLD PRICE	SHIPPING COST	SELLER FEES	TOTAL EXPENSE	PROFIT

NOTES

INVENTORY #			ITEM		BRAND	

DESCRIPTION	

SOURCE		LOCATION		COST	

CATEGORY WOMEN ☐ MEN ☐ KIDS ☐ **CONDITION** NEW WITH TAGS ☐ PREOWNED ☐

DETAILS	MATERIAL	
	STYLE	
	FLAWS	

SIZING	TAG SIZE		WAIST		SHOULDER	
	CHEST		SLEEVE		INSEAM	
	LENGTH		NECK		RISE	

DATE SOLD	LISTING PRICE	SOLD PRICE	SHIPPING COST	SELLER FEES	TOTAL EXPENSE	PROFIT

NOTES

INVENTORY #		ITEM		BRAND	
DESCRIPTION					
SOURCE		LOCATION		COST	
CATEGORY	WOMEN ☐ MEN ☐ KIDS ☐	CONDITION	NEW WITH TAGS ☐ PREOWNED ☐		

DETAILS	MATERIAL	
	STYLE	
	FLAWS	

SIZING	TAG SIZE		WAIST		SHOULDER	
	CHEST		SLEEVE		INSEAM	
	LENGTH		NECK		RISE	

DATE SOLD	LISTING PRICE	SOLD PRICE	SHIPPING COST	SELLER FEES	TOTAL EXPENSE	PROFIT

NOTES

INVENTORY #		ITEM		BRAND	
DESCRIPTION					
SOURCE		LOCATION		COST	
CATEGORY	WOMEN ☐ MEN ☐ KIDS ☐	CONDITION	NEW WITH TAGS ☐ PREOWNED ☐		

DETAILS	MATERIAL	
	STYLE	
	FLAWS	

SIZING	TAG SIZE		WAIST		SHOULDER	
	CHEST		SLEEVE		INSEAM	
	LENGTH		NECK		RISE	

DATE SOLD	LISTING PRICE	SOLD PRICE	SHIPPING COST	SELLER FEES	TOTAL EXPENSE	PROFIT

NOTES

INVENTORY #		ITEM		BRAND	

DESCRIPTION	

SOURCE		LOCATION		COST	

CATEGORY	WOMEN ☐ MEN ☐ KIDS ☐	CONDITION	NEW WITH TAGS ☐ PREOWNED ☐

DETAILS	MATERIAL	
	STYLE	
	FLAWS	

SIZING	TAG SIZE		WAIST		SHOULDER	
	CHEST		SLEEVE		INSEAM	
	LENGTH		NECK		RISE	

DATE SOLD	LISTING PRICE	SOLD PRICE	SHIPPING COST	SELLER FEES	TOTAL EXPENSE	PROFIT

NOTES

INVENTORY #		ITEM		BRAND	

DESCRIPTION	

SOURCE		LOCATION		COST	

CATEGORY	WOMEN ☐ MEN ☐ KIDS ☐	CONDITION	NEW WITH TAGS ☐ PREOWNED ☐

DETAILS	MATERIAL	
	STYLE	
	FLAWS	

SIZING	TAG SIZE		WAIST		SHOULDER	
	CHEST		SLEEVE		INSEAM	
	LENGTH		NECK		RISE	

DATE SOLD	LISTING PRICE	SOLD PRICE	SHIPPING COST	SELLER FEES	TOTAL EXPENSE	PROFIT

NOTES

INVENTORY #		ITEM		BRAND	
DESCRIPTION					
SOURCE		LOCATION		COST	
CATEGORY	WOMEN ☐ MEN ☐ KIDS ☐	CONDITION	NEW WITH TAGS ☐	PREOWNED ☐	

DETAILS	MATERIAL	
	STYLE	
	FLAWS	

SIZING	TAG SIZE		WAIST		SHOULDER	
	CHEST		SLEEVE		INSEAM	
	LENGTH		NECK		RISE	

DATE SOLD	LISTING PRICE	SOLD PRICE	SHIPPING COST	SELLER FEES	TOTAL EXPENSE	PROFIT

NOTES

INVENTORY #		ITEM		BRAND	
DESCRIPTION					
SOURCE		LOCATION		COST	
CATEGORY	WOMEN ☐ MEN ☐ KIDS ☐	CONDITION	NEW WITH TAGS ☐	PREOWNED ☐	

DETAILS	MATERIAL	
	STYLE	
	FLAWS	

SIZING	TAG SIZE		WAIST		SHOULDER	
	CHEST		SLEEVE		INSEAM	
	LENGTH		NECK		RISE	

DATE SOLD	LISTING PRICE	SOLD PRICE	SHIPPING COST	SELLER FEES	TOTAL EXPENSE	PROFIT

NOTES

INVENTORY #		ITEM		BRAND	

DESCRIPTION	

SOURCE		LOCATION		COST	

CATEGORY	WOMEN ☐ MEN ☐ KIDS ☐	CONDITION	NEW WITH TAGS ☐ PREOWNED ☐

DETAILS	MATERIAL	
	STYLE	
	FLAWS	

SIZING	TAG SIZE		WAIST		SHOULDER	
	CHEST		SLEEVE		INSEAM	
	LENGTH		NECK		RISE	

DATE SOLD	LISTING PRICE	SOLD PRICE	SHIPPING COST	SELLER FEES	TOTAL EXPENSE	PROFIT

NOTES

INVENTORY #		ITEM		BRAND	

DESCRIPTION	

SOURCE		LOCATION		COST	

CATEGORY	WOMEN ☐ MEN ☐ KIDS ☐	CONDITION	NEW WITH TAGS ☐ PREOWNED ☐

DETAILS	MATERIAL	
	STYLE	
	FLAWS	

SIZING	TAG SIZE		WAIST		SHOULDER	
	CHEST		SLEEVE		INSEAM	
	LENGTH		NECK		RISE	

DATE SOLD	LISTING PRICE	SOLD PRICE	SHIPPING COST	SELLER FEES	TOTAL EXPENSE	PROFIT

NOTES

INVENTORY #		ITEM		BRAND	

DESCRIPTION	

SOURCE		LOCATION		COST	

CATEGORY	WOMEN ☐ MEN ☐ KIDS ☐	CONDITION	NEW WITH TAGS ☐ PREOWNED ☐

DETAILS	MATERIAL	
	STYLE	
	FLAWS	

SIZING	TAG SIZE		WAIST		SHOULDER	
	CHEST		SLEEVE		INSEAM	
	LENGTH		NECK		RISE	

DATE SOLD	LISTING PRICE	SOLD PRICE	SHIPPING COST	SELLER FEES	TOTAL EXPENSE	PROFIT

NOTES

INVENTORY #		ITEM		BRAND	

DESCRIPTION	

SOURCE		LOCATION		COST	

CATEGORY	WOMEN ☐ MEN ☐ KIDS ☐	CONDITION	NEW WITH TAGS ☐ PREOWNED ☐

DETAILS	MATERIAL	
	STYLE	
	FLAWS	

SIZING	TAG SIZE		WAIST		SHOULDER	
	CHEST		SLEEVE		INSEAM	
	LENGTH		NECK		RISE	

DATE SOLD	LISTING PRICE	SOLD PRICE	SHIPPING COST	SELLER FEES	TOTAL EXPENSE	PROFIT

NOTES

INVENTORY #			ITEM		BRAND	

DESCRIPTION	

SOURCE		LOCATION		COST	

CATEGORY	WOMEN ☐ MEN ☐ KIDS ☐	CONDITION	NEW WITH TAGS ☐ PREOWNED ☐

DETAILS	MATERIAL	
	STYLE	
	FLAWS	

SIZING	TAG SIZE		WAIST		SHOULDER	
	CHEST		SLEEVE		INSEAM	
	LENGTH		NECK		RISE	

DATE SOLD	LISTING PRICE	SOLD PRICE	SHIPPING COST	SELLER FEES	TOTAL EXPENSE	PROFIT

NOTES

INVENTORY #			ITEM		BRAND	

DESCRIPTION	

SOURCE		LOCATION		COST	

CATEGORY	WOMEN ☐ MEN ☐ KIDS ☐	CONDITION	NEW WITH TAGS ☐ PREOWNED ☐

DETAILS	MATERIAL	
	STYLE	
	FLAWS	

SIZING	TAG SIZE		WAIST		SHOULDER	
	CHEST		SLEEVE		INSEAM	
	LENGTH		NECK		RISE	

DATE SOLD	LISTING PRICE	SOLD PRICE	SHIPPING COST	SELLER FEES	TOTAL EXPENSE	PROFIT

NOTES

INVENTORY #		ITEM		BRAND	
DESCRIPTION					
SOURCE		LOCATION		COST	
CATEGORY	WOMEN ☐ MEN ☐ KIDS ☐	CONDITION	NEW WITH TAGS ☐	PREOWNED ☐	

DETAILS	MATERIAL	
	STYLE	
	FLAWS	

SIZING	TAG SIZE		WAIST		SHOULDER	
	CHEST		SLEEVE		INSEAM	
	LENGTH		NECK		RISE	

DATE SOLD	LISTING PRICE	SOLD PRICE	SHIPPING COST	SELLER FEES	TOTAL EXPENSE	PROFIT

NOTES

INVENTORY #		ITEM		BRAND	
DESCRIPTION					
SOURCE		LOCATION		COST	
CATEGORY	WOMEN ☐ MEN ☐ KIDS ☐	CONDITION	NEW WITH TAGS ☐	PREOWNED ☐	

DETAILS	MATERIAL	
	STYLE	
	FLAWS	

SIZING	TAG SIZE		WAIST		SHOULDER	
	CHEST		SLEEVE		INSEAM	
	LENGTH		NECK		RISE	

DATE SOLD	LISTING PRICE	SOLD PRICE	SHIPPING COST	SELLER FEES	TOTAL EXPENSE	PROFIT

NOTES

INVENTORY #		ITEM		BRAND	
DESCRIPTION					
SOURCE		LOCATION		COST	

CATEGORY	WOMEN ☐ MEN ☐ KIDS ☐	CONDITION	NEW WITH TAGS ☐ PREOWNED ☐

DETAILS	MATERIAL	
	STYLE	
	FLAWS	

SIZING	TAG SIZE		WAIST		SHOULDER	
	CHEST		SLEEVE		INSEAM	
	LENGTH		NECK		RISE	

DATE SOLD	LISTING PRICE	SOLD PRICE	SHIPPING COST	SELLER FEES	TOTAL EXPENSE	PROFIT

NOTES

INVENTORY #		ITEM		BRAND	
DESCRIPTION					
SOURCE		LOCATION		COST	

CATEGORY	WOMEN ☐ MEN ☐ KIDS ☐	CONDITION	NEW WITH TAGS ☐ PREOWNED ☐

DETAILS	MATERIAL	
	STYLE	
	FLAWS	

SIZING	TAG SIZE		WAIST		SHOULDER	
	CHEST		SLEEVE		INSEAM	
	LENGTH		NECK		RISE	

DATE SOLD	LISTING PRICE	SOLD PRICE	SHIPPING COST	SELLER FEES	TOTAL EXPENSE	PROFIT

NOTES

INVENTORY #			ITEM			BRAND	

DESCRIPTION	

SOURCE		LOCATION		COST	

CATEGORY	WOMEN ☐ MEN ☐ KIDS ☐	CONDITION	NEW WITH TAGS ☐ PREOWNED ☐

DETAILS	MATERIAL	
	STYLE	
	FLAWS	

SIZING	TAG SIZE		WAIST		SHOULDER	
	CHEST		SLEEVE		INSEAM	
	LENGTH		NECK		RISE	

DATE SOLD	LISTING PRICE	SOLD PRICE	SHIPPING COST	SELLER FEES	TOTAL EXPENSE	PROFIT

NOTES

INVENTORY #			ITEM			BRAND	

DESCRIPTION	

SOURCE		LOCATION		COST	

CATEGORY	WOMEN ☐ MEN ☐ KIDS ☐	CONDITION	NEW WITH TAGS ☐ PREOWNED ☐

DETAILS	MATERIAL	
	STYLE	
	FLAWS	

SIZING	TAG SIZE		WAIST		SHOULDER	
	CHEST		SLEEVE		INSEAM	
	LENGTH		NECK		RISE	

DATE SOLD	LISTING PRICE	SOLD PRICE	SHIPPING COST	SELLER FEES	TOTAL EXPENSE	PROFIT

NOTES

INVENTORY #		ITEM		BRAND	

DESCRIPTION	

SOURCE		LOCATION		COST	

CATEGORY	WOMEN ☐ MEN ☐ KIDS ☐	CONDITION	NEW WITH TAGS ☐ PREOWNED ☐

DETAILS	MATERIAL	
	STYLE	
	FLAWS	

SIZING	TAG SIZE		WAIST		SHOULDER	
	CHEST		SLEEVE		INSEAM	
	LENGTH		NECK		RISE	

DATE SOLD	LISTING PRICE	SOLD PRICE	SHIPPING COST	SELLER FEES	TOTAL EXPENSE	PROFIT

NOTES

INVENTORY #		ITEM		BRAND	

DESCRIPTION	

SOURCE		LOCATION		COST	

CATEGORY	WOMEN ☐ MEN ☐ KIDS ☐	CONDITION	NEW WITH TAGS ☐ PREOWNED ☐

DETAILS	MATERIAL	
	STYLE	
	FLAWS	

SIZING	TAG SIZE		WAIST		SHOULDER	
	CHEST		SLEEVE		INSEAM	
	LENGTH		NECK		RISE	

DATE SOLD	LISTING PRICE	SOLD PRICE	SHIPPING COST	SELLER FEES	TOTAL EXPENSE	PROFIT

NOTES

INVENTORY #		ITEM		BRAND	
DESCRIPTION					
SOURCE		LOCATION		COST	
CATEGORY	WOMEN ☐ MEN ☐ KIDS ☐	CONDITION	NEW WITH TAGS ☐	PREOWNED ☐	

DETAILS	MATERIAL	
	STYLE	
	FLAWS	

SIZING	TAG SIZE		WAIST		SHOULDER	
	CHEST		SLEEVE		INSEAM	
	LENGTH		NECK		RISE	

DATE SOLD	LISTING PRICE	SOLD PRICE	SHIPPING COST	SELLER FEES	TOTAL EXPENSE	PROFIT

NOTES

INVENTORY #		ITEM		BRAND	
DESCRIPTION					
SOURCE		LOCATION		COST	
CATEGORY	WOMEN ☐ MEN ☐ KIDS ☐	CONDITION	NEW WITH TAGS ☐	PREOWNED ☐	

DETAILS	MATERIAL	
	STYLE	
	FLAWS	

SIZING	TAG SIZE		WAIST		SHOULDER	
	CHEST		SLEEVE		INSEAM	
	LENGTH		NECK		RISE	

DATE SOLD	LISTING PRICE	SOLD PRICE	SHIPPING COST	SELLER FEES	TOTAL EXPENSE	PROFIT

NOTES

INVENTORY #			ITEM		BRAND		

DESCRIPTION	

SOURCE		LOCATION		COST	

CATEGORY	WOMEN ☐ MEN ☐ KIDS ☐	CONDITION	NEW WITH TAGS ☐ PREOWNED ☐

DETAILS	MATERIAL	
	STYLE	
	FLAWS	

SIZING	TAG SIZE		WAIST		SHOULDER	
	CHEST		SLEEVE		INSEAM	
	LENGTH		NECK		RISE	

DATE SOLD	LISTING PRICE	SOLD PRICE	SHIPPING COST	SELLER FEES	TOTAL EXPENSE	PROFIT

NOTES

INVENTORY #			ITEM		BRAND		

DESCRIPTION	

SOURCE		LOCATION		COST	

CATEGORY	WOMEN ☐ MEN ☐ KIDS ☐	CONDITION	NEW WITH TAGS ☐ PREOWNED ☐

DETAILS	MATERIAL	
	STYLE	
	FLAWS	

SIZING	TAG SIZE		WAIST		SHOULDER	
	CHEST		SLEEVE		INSEAM	
	LENGTH		NECK		RISE	

DATE SOLD	LISTING PRICE	SOLD PRICE	SHIPPING COST	SELLER FEES	TOTAL EXPENSE	PROFIT

NOTES

INVENTORY #		ITEM		BRAND	

DESCRIPTION	

SOURCE		LOCATION		COST	

CATEGORY	WOMEN ☐ MEN ☐ KIDS ☐	CONDITION	NEW WITH TAGS ☐ PREOWNED ☐

DETAILS	MATERIAL	
	STYLE	
	FLAWS	

SIZING	TAG SIZE		WAIST		SHOULDER	
	CHEST		SLEEVE		INSEAM	
	LENGTH		NECK		RISE	

DATE SOLD	LISTING PRICE	SOLD PRICE	SHIPPING COST	SELLER FEES	TOTAL EXPENSE	PROFIT

NOTES

INVENTORY #		ITEM		BRAND	

DESCRIPTION	

SOURCE		LOCATION		COST	

CATEGORY	WOMEN ☐ MEN ☐ KIDS ☐	CONDITION	NEW WITH TAGS ☐ PREOWNED ☐

DETAILS	MATERIAL	
	STYLE	
	FLAWS	

SIZING	TAG SIZE		WAIST		SHOULDER	
	CHEST		SLEEVE		INSEAM	
	LENGTH		NECK		RISE	

DATE SOLD	LISTING PRICE	SOLD PRICE	SHIPPING COST	SELLER FEES	TOTAL EXPENSE	PROFIT

NOTES

INVENTORY #		ITEM		BRAND	

DESCRIPTION	

SOURCE		LOCATION		COST	

CATEGORY	WOMEN ☐ MEN ☐ KIDS ☐	CONDITION	NEW WITH TAGS ☐ PREOWNED ☐

DETAILS	MATERIAL	
	STYLE	
	FLAWS	

SIZING	TAG SIZE		WAIST		SHOULDER	
	CHEST		SLEEVE		INSEAM	
	LENGTH		NECK		RISE	

DATE SOLD	LISTING PRICE	SOLD PRICE	SHIPPING COST	SELLER FEES	TOTAL EXPENSE	PROFIT

NOTES

INVENTORY #		ITEM		BRAND	

DESCRIPTION	

SOURCE		LOCATION		COST	

CATEGORY	WOMEN ☐ MEN ☐ KIDS ☐	CONDITION	NEW WITH TAGS ☐ PREOWNED ☐

DETAILS	MATERIAL	
	STYLE	
	FLAWS	

SIZING	TAG SIZE		WAIST		SHOULDER	
	CHEST		SLEEVE		INSEAM	
	LENGTH		NECK		RISE	

DATE SOLD	LISTING PRICE	SOLD PRICE	SHIPPING COST	SELLER FEES	TOTAL EXPENSE	PROFIT

NOTES

INVENTORY #		ITEM		BRAND	

DESCRIPTION	

SOURCE		LOCATION		COST	

CATEGORY WOMEN ☐ MEN ☐ KIDS ☐ CONDITION NEW WITH TAGS ☐ PREOWNED ☐

DETAILS	MATERIAL	
	STYLE	
	FLAWS	

SIZING	TAG SIZE		WAIST		SHOULDER	
	CHEST		SLEEVE		INSEAM	
	LENGTH		NECK		RISE	

DATE SOLD	LISTING PRICE	SOLD PRICE	SHIPPING COST	SELLER FEES	TOTAL EXPENSE	PROFIT

NOTES

INVENTORY #		ITEM		BRAND	

DESCRIPTION	

SOURCE		LOCATION		COST	

CATEGORY WOMEN ☐ MEN ☐ KIDS ☐ CONDITION NEW WITH TAGS ☐ PREOWNED ☐

DETAILS	MATERIAL	
	STYLE	
	FLAWS	

SIZING	TAG SIZE		WAIST		SHOULDER	
	CHEST		SLEEVE		INSEAM	
	LENGTH		NECK		RISE	

DATE SOLD	LISTING PRICE	SOLD PRICE	SHIPPING COST	SELLER FEES	TOTAL EXPENSE	PROFIT

NOTES

INVENTORY #		ITEM		BRAND	

DESCRIPTION	

SOURCE		LOCATION		COST	

CATEGORY	WOMEN ☐ MEN ☐ KIDS ☐	CONDITION	NEW WITH TAGS ☐ PREOWNED ☐

DETAILS	MATERIAL	
	STYLE	
	FLAWS	

SIZING	TAG SIZE		WAIST		SHOULDER	
	CHEST		SLEEVE		INSEAM	
	LENGTH		NECK		RISE	

DATE SOLD	LISTING PRICE	SOLD PRICE	SHIPPING COST	SELLER FEES	TOTAL EXPENSE	PROFIT

NOTES

INVENTORY #		ITEM		BRAND	

DESCRIPTION	

SOURCE		LOCATION		COST	

CATEGORY	WOMEN ☐ MEN ☐ KIDS ☐	CONDITION	NEW WITH TAGS ☐ PREOWNED ☐

DETAILS	MATERIAL	
	STYLE	
	FLAWS	

SIZING	TAG SIZE		WAIST		SHOULDER	
	CHEST		SLEEVE		INSEAM	
	LENGTH		NECK		RISE	

DATE SOLD	LISTING PRICE	SOLD PRICE	SHIPPING COST	SELLER FEES	TOTAL EXPENSE	PROFIT

NOTES

INVENTORY #			ITEM		BRAND	

DESCRIPTION	

SOURCE		LOCATION		COST	

CATEGORY	WOMEN ☐ MEN ☐ KIDS ☐	CONDITION	NEW WITH TAGS ☐ PREOWNED ☐

DETAILS	MATERIAL	
	STYLE	
	FLAWS	

SIZING	TAG SIZE		WAIST		SHOULDER	
	CHEST		SLEEVE		INSEAM	
	LENGTH		NECK		RISE	

DATE SOLD	LISTING PRICE	SOLD PRICE	SHIPPING COST	SELLER FEES	TOTAL EXPENSE	PROFIT

NOTES

INVENTORY #			ITEM		BRAND	

DESCRIPTION	

SOURCE		LOCATION		COST	

CATEGORY	WOMEN ☐ MEN ☐ KIDS ☐	CONDITION	NEW WITH TAGS ☐ PREOWNED ☐

DETAILS	MATERIAL	
	STYLE	
	FLAWS	

SIZING	TAG SIZE		WAIST		SHOULDER	
	CHEST		SLEEVE		INSEAM	
	LENGTH		NECK		RISE	

DATE SOLD	LISTING PRICE	SOLD PRICE	SHIPPING COST	SELLER FEES	TOTAL EXPENSE	PROFIT

NOTES

INVENTORY #			ITEM		BRAND	

DESCRIPTION	

SOURCE		LOCATION		COST	

CATEGORY	WOMEN ☐ MEN ☐ KIDS ☐	CONDITION	NEW WITH TAGS ☐ PREOWNED ☐

DETAILS	MATERIAL	
	STYLE	
	FLAWS	

SIZING	TAG SIZE		WAIST		SHOULDER	
	CHEST		SLEEVE		INSEAM	
	LENGTH		NECK		RISE	

DATE SOLD	LISTING PRICE	SOLD PRICE	SHIPPING COST	SELLER FEES	TOTAL EXPENSE	PROFIT

NOTES

INVENTORY #			ITEM		BRAND	

DESCRIPTION	

SOURCE		LOCATION		COST	

CATEGORY	WOMEN ☐ MEN ☐ KIDS ☐	CONDITION	NEW WITH TAGS ☐ PREOWNED ☐

DETAILS	MATERIAL	
	STYLE	
	FLAWS	

SIZING	TAG SIZE		WAIST		SHOULDER	
	CHEST		SLEEVE		INSEAM	
	LENGTH		NECK		RISE	

DATE SOLD	LISTING PRICE	SOLD PRICE	SHIPPING COST	SELLER FEES	TOTAL EXPENSE	PROFIT

NOTES

INVENTORY #		ITEM		BRAND	

DESCRIPTION	

SOURCE		LOCATION		COST	

CATEGORY	WOMEN ☐ MEN ☐ KIDS ☐	CONDITION	NEW WITH TAGS ☐ PREOWNED ☐

DETAILS	MATERIAL	
	STYLE	
	FLAWS	

SIZING	TAG SIZE		WAIST		SHOULDER	
	CHEST		SLEEVE		INSEAM	
	LENGTH		NECK		RISE	

DATE SOLD	LISTING PRICE	SOLD PRICE	SHIPPING COST	SELLER FEES	TOTAL EXPENSE	PROFIT

NOTES

INVENTORY #		ITEM		BRAND	

DESCRIPTION	

SOURCE		LOCATION		COST	

CATEGORY	WOMEN ☐ MEN ☐ KIDS ☐	CONDITION	NEW WITH TAGS ☐ PREOWNED ☐

DETAILS	MATERIAL	
	STYLE	
	FLAWS	

SIZING	TAG SIZE		WAIST		SHOULDER	
	CHEST		SLEEVE		INSEAM	
	LENGTH		NECK		RISE	

DATE SOLD	LISTING PRICE	SOLD PRICE	SHIPPING COST	SELLER FEES	TOTAL EXPENSE	PROFIT

NOTES

INVENTORY #		ITEM		BRAND	

DESCRIPTION	

SOURCE		LOCATION		COST	

CATEGORY	WOMEN ☐ MEN ☐ KIDS ☐	CONDITION	NEW WITH TAGS ☐ PREOWNED ☐

DETAILS	MATERIAL	
	STYLE	
	FLAWS	

SIZING	TAG SIZE		WAIST		SHOULDER	
	CHEST		SLEEVE		INSEAM	
	LENGTH		NECK		RISE	

DATE SOLD	LISTING PRICE	SOLD PRICE	SHIPPING COST	SELLER FEES	TOTAL EXPENSE	PROFIT

NOTES

INVENTORY #		ITEM		BRAND	

DESCRIPTION	

SOURCE		LOCATION		COST	

CATEGORY	WOMEN ☐ MEN ☐ KIDS ☐	CONDITION	NEW WITH TAGS ☐ PREOWNED ☐

DETAILS	MATERIAL	
	STYLE	
	FLAWS	

SIZING	TAG SIZE		WAIST		SHOULDER	
	CHEST		SLEEVE		INSEAM	
	LENGTH		NECK		RISE	

DATE SOLD	LISTING PRICE	SOLD PRICE	SHIPPING COST	SELLER FEES	TOTAL EXPENSE	PROFIT

NOTES

INVENTORY #		ITEM		BRAND	

DESCRIPTION	

SOURCE		LOCATION		COST	

CATEGORY	WOMEN ☐ MEN ☐ KIDS ☐	CONDITION	NEW WITH TAGS ☐ PREOWNED ☐

DETAILS	MATERIAL	
	STYLE	
	FLAWS	

SIZING	TAG SIZE		WAIST		SHOULDER	
	CHEST		SLEEVE		INSEAM	
	LENGTH		NECK		RISE	

DATE SOLD	LISTING PRICE	SOLD PRICE	SHIPPING COST	SELLER FEES	TOTAL EXPENSE	PROFIT

NOTES

INVENTORY #		ITEM		BRAND	

DESCRIPTION	

SOURCE		LOCATION		COST	

CATEGORY	WOMEN ☐ MEN ☐ KIDS ☐	CONDITION	NEW WITH TAGS ☐ PREOWNED ☐

DETAILS	MATERIAL	
	STYLE	
	FLAWS	

SIZING	TAG SIZE		WAIST		SHOULDER	
	CHEST		SLEEVE		INSEAM	
	LENGTH		NECK		RISE	

DATE SOLD	LISTING PRICE	SOLD PRICE	SHIPPING COST	SELLER FEES	TOTAL EXPENSE	PROFIT

NOTES

INVENTORY #		ITEM		BRAND	
DESCRIPTION					
SOURCE		LOCATION		COST	
CATEGORY	WOMEN ☐ MEN ☐ KIDS ☐	CONDITION	NEW WITH TAGS ☐	PREOWNED ☐	

DETAILS	MATERIAL	
	STYLE	
	FLAWS	

SIZING	TAG SIZE		WAIST		SHOULDER	
	CHEST		SLEEVE		INSEAM	
	LENGTH		NECK		RISE	

DATE SOLD	LISTING PRICE	SOLD PRICE	SHIPPING COST	SELLER FEES	TOTAL EXPENSE	PROFIT

NOTES

INVENTORY #		ITEM		BRAND	
DESCRIPTION					
SOURCE		LOCATION		COST	
CATEGORY	WOMEN ☐ MEN ☐ KIDS ☐	CONDITION	NEW WITH TAGS ☐	PREOWNED ☐	

DETAILS	MATERIAL	
	STYLE	
	FLAWS	

SIZING	TAG SIZE		WAIST		SHOULDER	
	CHEST		SLEEVE		INSEAM	
	LENGTH		NECK		RISE	

DATE SOLD	LISTING PRICE	SOLD PRICE	SHIPPING COST	SELLER FEES	TOTAL EXPENSE	PROFIT

NOTES

INVENTORY #		ITEM		BRAND	
DESCRIPTION					

SOURCE		LOCATION		COST	

CATEGORY	WOMEN ☐ MEN ☐ KIDS ☐	CONDITION	NEW WITH TAGS ☐	PREOWNED ☐

DETAILS	MATERIAL	
	STYLE	
	FLAWS	

SIZING	TAG SIZE		WAIST		SHOULDER	
	CHEST		SLEEVE		INSEAM	
	LENGTH		NECK		RISE	

DATE SOLD	LISTING PRICE	SOLD PRICE	SHIPPING COST	SELLER FEES	TOTAL EXPENSE	PROFIT

NOTES

INVENTORY #		ITEM		BRAND	
DESCRIPTION					

SOURCE		LOCATION		COST	

CATEGORY	WOMEN ☐ MEN ☐ KIDS ☐	CONDITION	NEW WITH TAGS ☐	PREOWNED ☐

DETAILS	MATERIAL	
	STYLE	
	FLAWS	

SIZING	TAG SIZE		WAIST		SHOULDER	
	CHEST		SLEEVE		INSEAM	
	LENGTH		NECK		RISE	

DATE SOLD	LISTING PRICE	SOLD PRICE	SHIPPING COST	SELLER FEES	TOTAL EXPENSE	PROFIT

NOTES

INVENTORY #			ITEM		BRAND	

DESCRIPTION	

SOURCE		LOCATION		COST	

CATEGORY	WOMEN ☐ MEN ☐ KIDS ☐	CONDITION	NEW WITH TAGS ☐ PREOWNED ☐

DETAILS	MATERIAL	
	STYLE	
	FLAWS	

SIZING	TAG SIZE		WAIST		SHOULDER	
	CHEST		SLEEVE		INSEAM	
	LENGTH		NECK		RISE	

DATE SOLD	LISTING PRICE	SOLD PRICE	SHIPPING COST	SELLER FEES	TOTAL EXPENSE	PROFIT

NOTES

INVENTORY #			ITEM		BRAND	

DESCRIPTION	

SOURCE		LOCATION		COST	

CATEGORY	WOMEN ☐ MEN ☐ KIDS ☐	CONDITION	NEW WITH TAGS ☐ PREOWNED ☐

DETAILS	MATERIAL	
	STYLE	
	FLAWS	

SIZING	TAG SIZE		WAIST		SHOULDER	
	CHEST		SLEEVE		INSEAM	
	LENGTH		NECK		RISE	

DATE SOLD	LISTING PRICE	SOLD PRICE	SHIPPING COST	SELLER FEES	TOTAL EXPENSE	PROFIT

NOTES

INVENTORY #		ITEM		BRAND	
DESCRIPTION					

SOURCE		LOCATION		COST	

CATEGORY	WOMEN ☐ MEN ☐ KIDS ☐	CONDITION	NEW WITH TAGS ☐ PREOWNED ☐

DETAILS	MATERIAL	
	STYLE	
	FLAWS	

SIZING	TAG SIZE		WAIST		SHOULDER	
	CHEST		SLEEVE		INSEAM	
	LENGTH		NECK		RISE	

DATE SOLD	LISTING PRICE	SOLD PRICE	SHIPPING COST	SELLER FEES	TOTAL EXPENSE	PROFIT

NOTES

INVENTORY #		ITEM		BRAND	
DESCRIPTION					

SOURCE		LOCATION		COST	

CATEGORY	WOMEN ☐ MEN ☐ KIDS ☐	CONDITION	NEW WITH TAGS ☐ PREOWNED ☐

DETAILS	MATERIAL	
	STYLE	
	FLAWS	

SIZING	TAG SIZE		WAIST		SHOULDER	
	CHEST		SLEEVE		INSEAM	
	LENGTH		NECK		RISE	

DATE SOLD	LISTING PRICE	SOLD PRICE	SHIPPING COST	SELLER FEES	TOTAL EXPENSE	PROFIT

NOTES

INVENTORY #			ITEM		BRAND	

DESCRIPTION	

SOURCE		LOCATION		COST	

CATEGORY	WOMEN ☐ MEN ☐ KIDS ☐	CONDITION	NEW WITH TAGS ☐ PREOWNED ☐

DETAILS	MATERIAL	
	STYLE	
	FLAWS	

SIZING	TAG SIZE		WAIST		SHOULDER	
	CHEST		SLEEVE		INSEAM	
	LENGTH		NECK		RISE	

DATE SOLD	LISTING PRICE	SOLD PRICE	SHIPPING COST	SELLER FEES	TOTAL EXPENSE	PROFIT

NOTES

INVENTORY #			ITEM		BRAND	

DESCRIPTION	

SOURCE		LOCATION		COST	

CATEGORY	WOMEN ☐ MEN ☐ KIDS ☐	CONDITION	NEW WITH TAGS ☐ PREOWNED ☐

DETAILS	MATERIAL	
	STYLE	
	FLAWS	

SIZING	TAG SIZE		WAIST		SHOULDER	
	CHEST		SLEEVE		INSEAM	
	LENGTH		NECK		RISE	

DATE SOLD	LISTING PRICE	SOLD PRICE	SHIPPING COST	SELLER FEES	TOTAL EXPENSE	PROFIT

NOTES

INVENTORY #		ITEM		BRAND	

DESCRIPTION	

SOURCE		LOCATION		COST	

CATEGORY	WOMEN ☐ MEN ☐ KIDS ☐	CONDITION	NEW WITH TAGS ☐ PREOWNED ☐

DETAILS	MATERIAL	
	STYLE	
	FLAWS	

SIZING	TAG SIZE		WAIST		SHOULDER	
	CHEST		SLEEVE		INSEAM	
	LENGTH		NECK		RISE	

DATE SOLD	LISTING PRICE	SOLD PRICE	SHIPPING COST	SELLER FEES	TOTAL EXPENSE	PROFIT

NOTES

INVENTORY #		ITEM		BRAND	

DESCRIPTION	

SOURCE		LOCATION		COST	

CATEGORY	WOMEN ☐ MEN ☐ KIDS ☐	CONDITION	NEW WITH TAGS ☐ PREOWNED ☐

DETAILS	MATERIAL	
	STYLE	
	FLAWS	

SIZING	TAG SIZE		WAIST		SHOULDER	
	CHEST		SLEEVE		INSEAM	
	LENGTH		NECK		RISE	

DATE SOLD	LISTING PRICE	SOLD PRICE	SHIPPING COST	SELLER FEES	TOTAL EXPENSE	PROFIT

NOTES

INVENTORY #		ITEM		BRAND	
DESCRIPTION					
SOURCE		LOCATION		COST	
CATEGORY	WOMEN ☐ MEN ☐ KIDS ☐	CONDITION	NEW WITH TAGS ☐ PREOWNED ☐		

DETAILS	MATERIAL	
	STYLE	
	FLAWS	

SIZING	TAG SIZE		WAIST		SHOULDER	
	CHEST		SLEEVE		INSEAM	
	LENGTH		NECK		RISE	

DATE SOLD	LISTING PRICE	SOLD PRICE	SHIPPING COST	SELLER FEES	TOTAL EXPENSE	PROFIT

NOTES

INVENTORY #		ITEM		BRAND	
DESCRIPTION					
SOURCE		LOCATION		COST	
CATEGORY	WOMEN ☐ MEN ☐ KIDS ☐	CONDITION	NEW WITH TAGS ☐ PREOWNED ☐		

DETAILS	MATERIAL	
	STYLE	
	FLAWS	

SIZING	TAG SIZE		WAIST		SHOULDER	
	CHEST		SLEEVE		INSEAM	
	LENGTH		NECK		RISE	

DATE SOLD	LISTING PRICE	SOLD PRICE	SHIPPING COST	SELLER FEES	TOTAL EXPENSE	PROFIT

NOTES

INVENTORY #		ITEM		BRAND	

DESCRIPTION	

SOURCE		LOCATION		COST	

CATEGORY	WOMEN ☐ MEN ☐ KIDS ☐	CONDITION	NEW WITH TAGS ☐ PREOWNED ☐

DETAILS	MATERIAL	
	STYLE	
	FLAWS	

SIZING	TAG SIZE		WAIST		SHOULDER	
	CHEST		SLEEVE		INSEAM	
	LENGTH		NECK		RISE	

DATE SOLD	LISTING PRICE	SOLD PRICE	SHIPPING COST	SELLER FEES	TOTAL EXPENSE	PROFIT

NOTES

INVENTORY #		ITEM		BRAND	

DESCRIPTION	

SOURCE		LOCATION		COST	

CATEGORY	WOMEN ☐ MEN ☐ KIDS ☐	CONDITION	NEW WITH TAGS ☐ PREOWNED ☐

DETAILS	MATERIAL	
	STYLE	
	FLAWS	

SIZING	TAG SIZE		WAIST		SHOULDER	
	CHEST		SLEEVE		INSEAM	
	LENGTH		NECK		RISE	

DATE SOLD	LISTING PRICE	SOLD PRICE	SHIPPING COST	SELLER FEES	TOTAL EXPENSE	PROFIT

NOTES

INVENTORY #		ITEM		BRAND	
DESCRIPTION					
SOURCE		LOCATION		COST	
CATEGORY	WOMEN ☐ MEN ☐ KIDS ☐	CONDITION	NEW WITH TAGS ☐	PREOWNED ☐	

DETAILS	MATERIAL	
	STYLE	
	FLAWS	

SIZING	TAG SIZE		WAIST		SHOULDER	
	CHEST		SLEEVE		INSEAM	
	LENGTH		NECK		RISE	

DATE SOLD	LISTING PRICE	SOLD PRICE	SHIPPING COST	SELLER FEES	TOTAL EXPENSE	PROFIT

NOTES

INVENTORY #		ITEM		BRAND	
DESCRIPTION					
SOURCE		LOCATION		COST	
CATEGORY	WOMEN ☐ MEN ☐ KIDS ☐	CONDITION	NEW WITH TAGS ☐	PREOWNED ☐	

DETAILS	MATERIAL	
	STYLE	
	FLAWS	

SIZING	TAG SIZE		WAIST		SHOULDER	
	CHEST		SLEEVE		INSEAM	
	LENGTH		NECK		RISE	

DATE SOLD	LISTING PRICE	SOLD PRICE	SHIPPING COST	SELLER FEES	TOTAL EXPENSE	PROFIT

NOTES

INVENTORY #		ITEM		BRAND	

DESCRIPTION	

SOURCE		LOCATION		COST	

CATEGORY WOMEN ☐ MEN ☐ KIDS ☐ **CONDITION** NEW WITH TAGS ☐ PREOWNED ☐

DETAILS	MATERIAL	
	STYLE	
	FLAWS	

SIZING	TAG SIZE		WAIST		SHOULDER	
	CHEST		SLEEVE		INSEAM	
	LENGTH		NECK		RISE	

DATE SOLD	LISTING PRICE	SOLD PRICE	SHIPPING COST	SELLER FEES	TOTAL EXPENSE	PROFIT

NOTES

INVENTORY #		ITEM		BRAND	

DESCRIPTION	

SOURCE		LOCATION		COST	

CATEGORY WOMEN ☐ MEN ☐ KIDS ☐ **CONDITION** NEW WITH TAGS ☐ PREOWNED ☐

DETAILS	MATERIAL	
	STYLE	
	FLAWS	

SIZING	TAG SIZE		WAIST		SHOULDER	
	CHEST		SLEEVE		INSEAM	
	LENGTH		NECK		RISE	

DATE SOLD	LISTING PRICE	SOLD PRICE	SHIPPING COST	SELLER FEES	TOTAL EXPENSE	PROFIT

NOTES

INVENTORY #		ITEM		BRAND	

DESCRIPTION	

SOURCE		LOCATION		COST	

CATEGORY	WOMEN ☐ MEN ☐ KIDS ☐	CONDITION	NEW WITH TAGS ☐ PREOWNED ☐

DETAILS	MATERIAL	
	STYLE	
	FLAWS	

SIZING	TAG SIZE		WAIST		SHOULDER	
	CHEST		SLEEVE		INSEAM	
	LENGTH		NECK		RISE	

DATE SOLD	LISTING PRICE	SOLD PRICE	SHIPPING COST	SELLER FEES	TOTAL EXPENSE	PROFIT

NOTES

INVENTORY #		ITEM		BRAND	

DESCRIPTION	

SOURCE		LOCATION		COST	

CATEGORY	WOMEN ☐ MEN ☐ KIDS ☐	CONDITION	NEW WITH TAGS ☐ PREOWNED ☐

DETAILS	MATERIAL	
	STYLE	
	FLAWS	

SIZING	TAG SIZE		WAIST		SHOULDER	
	CHEST		SLEEVE		INSEAM	
	LENGTH		NECK		RISE	

DATE SOLD	LISTING PRICE	SOLD PRICE	SHIPPING COST	SELLER FEES	TOTAL EXPENSE	PROFIT

NOTES

INVENTORY #			ITEM		BRAND	
DESCRIPTION						
SOURCE			LOCATION		COST	
CATEGORY	WOMEN ☐	MEN ☐	KIDS ☐	CONDITION	NEW WITH TAGS ☐	PREOWNED ☐

DETAILS	MATERIAL	
	STYLE	
	FLAWS	

SIZING	TAG SIZE		WAIST		SHOULDER	
	CHEST		SLEEVE		INSEAM	
	LENGTH		NECK		RISE	

DATE SOLD	LISTING PRICE	SOLD PRICE	SHIPPING COST	SELLER FEES	TOTAL EXPENSE	PROFIT

NOTES

INVENTORY #			ITEM		BRAND	
DESCRIPTION						
SOURCE			LOCATION		COST	
CATEGORY	WOMEN ☐	MEN ☐	KIDS ☐	CONDITION	NEW WITH TAGS ☐	PREOWNED ☐

DETAILS	MATERIAL	
	STYLE	
	FLAWS	

SIZING	TAG SIZE		WAIST		SHOULDER	
	CHEST		SLEEVE		INSEAM	
	LENGTH		NECK		RISE	

DATE SOLD	LISTING PRICE	SOLD PRICE	SHIPPING COST	SELLER FEES	TOTAL EXPENSE	PROFIT

NOTES

INVENTORY #			ITEM		BRAND	

DESCRIPTION	

SOURCE		LOCATION		COST	

CATEGORY WOMEN ☐ MEN ☐ KIDS ☐ **CONDITION** NEW WITH TAGS ☐ PREOWNED ☐

DETAILS	MATERIAL	
	STYLE	
	FLAWS	

SIZING	TAG SIZE		WAIST		SHOULDER	
	CHEST		SLEEVE		INSEAM	
	LENGTH		NECK		RISE	

DATE SOLD	LISTING PRICE	SOLD PRICE	SHIPPING COST	SELLER FEES	TOTAL EXPENSE	PROFIT

NOTES

INVENTORY #			ITEM		BRAND	

DESCRIPTION	

SOURCE		LOCATION		COST	

CATEGORY WOMEN ☐ MEN ☐ KIDS ☐ **CONDITION** NEW WITH TAGS ☐ PREOWNED ☐

DETAILS	MATERIAL	
	STYLE	
	FLAWS	

SIZING	TAG SIZE		WAIST		SHOULDER	
	CHEST		SLEEVE		INSEAM	
	LENGTH		NECK		RISE	

DATE SOLD	LISTING PRICE	SOLD PRICE	SHIPPING COST	SELLER FEES	TOTAL EXPENSE	PROFIT

NOTES

INVENTORY #		ITEM		BRAND	

DESCRIPTION	

SOURCE		LOCATION		COST	

CATEGORY	WOMEN ☐ MEN ☐ KIDS ☐	CONDITION	NEW WITH TAGS ☐ PREOWNED ☐

DETAILS	MATERIAL	
	STYLE	
	FLAWS	

SIZING	TAG SIZE		WAIST		SHOULDER	
	CHEST		SLEEVE		INSEAM	
	LENGTH		NECK		RISE	

DATE SOLD	LISTING PRICE	SOLD PRICE	SHIPPING COST	SELLER FEES	TOTAL EXPENSE	PROFIT

NOTES

INVENTORY #		ITEM		BRAND	

DESCRIPTION	

SOURCE		LOCATION		COST	

CATEGORY	WOMEN ☐ MEN ☐ KIDS ☐	CONDITION	NEW WITH TAGS ☐ PREOWNED ☐

DETAILS	MATERIAL	
	STYLE	
	FLAWS	

SIZING	TAG SIZE		WAIST		SHOULDER	
	CHEST		SLEEVE		INSEAM	
	LENGTH		NECK		RISE	

DATE SOLD	LISTING PRICE	SOLD PRICE	SHIPPING COST	SELLER FEES	TOTAL EXPENSE	PROFIT

NOTES

INVENTORY #			ITEM			BRAND	

DESCRIPTION	

SOURCE		LOCATION		COST	

CATEGORY	WOMEN ☐ MEN ☐ KIDS ☐	CONDITION	NEW WITH TAGS ☐ PREOWNED ☐

DETAILS	MATERIAL	
	STYLE	
	FLAWS	

SIZING	TAG SIZE		WAIST		SHOULDER	
	CHEST		SLEEVE		INSEAM	
	LENGTH		NECK		RISE	

DATE SOLD	LISTING PRICE	SOLD PRICE	SHIPPING COST	SELLER FEES	TOTAL EXPENSE	PROFIT

NOTES

INVENTORY #			ITEM			BRAND	

DESCRIPTION	

SOURCE		LOCATION		COST	

CATEGORY	WOMEN ☐ MEN ☐ KIDS ☐	CONDITION	NEW WITH TAGS ☐ PREOWNED ☐

DETAILS	MATERIAL	
	STYLE	
	FLAWS	

SIZING	TAG SIZE		WAIST		SHOULDER	
	CHEST		SLEEVE		INSEAM	
	LENGTH		NECK		RISE	

DATE SOLD	LISTING PRICE	SOLD PRICE	SHIPPING COST	SELLER FEES	TOTAL EXPENSE	PROFIT

NOTES

INVENTORY #			ITEM			BRAND	
DESCRIPTION							

SOURCE		LOCATION		COST	

CATEGORY	WOMEN ☐ MEN ☐ KIDS ☐	CONDITION	NEW WITH TAGS ☐ PREOWNED ☐

DETAILS	MATERIAL	
	STYLE	
	FLAWS	

SIZING	TAG SIZE		WAIST		SHOULDER	
	CHEST		SLEEVE		INSEAM	
	LENGTH		NECK		RISE	

DATE SOLD	LISTING PRICE	SOLD PRICE	SHIPPING COST	SELLER FEES	TOTAL EXPENSE	PROFIT

NOTES

INVENTORY #			ITEM			BRAND	
DESCRIPTION							

SOURCE		LOCATION		COST	

CATEGORY	WOMEN ☐ MEN ☐ KIDS ☐	CONDITION	NEW WITH TAGS ☐ PREOWNED ☐

DETAILS	MATERIAL	
	STYLE	
	FLAWS	

SIZING	TAG SIZE		WAIST		SHOULDER	
	CHEST		SLEEVE		INSEAM	
	LENGTH		NECK		RISE	

DATE SOLD	LISTING PRICE	SOLD PRICE	SHIPPING COST	SELLER FEES	TOTAL EXPENSE	PROFIT

NOTES

INVENTORY #		ITEM		BRAND	
DESCRIPTION					

SOURCE		LOCATION		COST	

CATEGORY	WOMEN ☐ MEN ☐ KIDS ☐	CONDITION	NEW WITH TAGS ☐ PREOWNED ☐

DETAILS	MATERIAL	
	STYLE	
	FLAWS	

SIZING	TAG SIZE		WAIST		SHOULDER	
	CHEST		SLEEVE		INSEAM	
	LENGTH		NECK		RISE	

DATE SOLD	LISTING PRICE	SOLD PRICE	SHIPPING COST	SELLER FEES	TOTAL EXPENSE	PROFIT

NOTES

INVENTORY #		ITEM		BRAND	
DESCRIPTION					

SOURCE		LOCATION		COST	

CATEGORY	WOMEN ☐ MEN ☐ KIDS ☐	CONDITION	NEW WITH TAGS ☐ PREOWNED ☐

DETAILS	MATERIAL	
	STYLE	
	FLAWS	

SIZING	TAG SIZE		WAIST		SHOULDER	
	CHEST		SLEEVE		INSEAM	
	LENGTH		NECK		RISE	

DATE SOLD	LISTING PRICE	SOLD PRICE	SHIPPING COST	SELLER FEES	TOTAL EXPENSE	PROFIT

NOTES

INVENTORY #			ITEM			BRAND	
DESCRIPTION							
SOURCE			LOCATION			COST	
CATEGORY	WOMEN ☐	MEN ☐	KIDS ☐	CONDITION	NEW WITH TAGS ☐	PREOWNED ☐	

DETAILS	MATERIAL	
	STYLE	
	FLAWS	

SIZING	TAG SIZE		WAIST		SHOULDER	
	CHEST		SLEEVE		INSEAM	
	LENGTH		NECK		RISE	

DATE SOLD	LISTING PRICE	SOLD PRICE	SHIPPING COST	SELLER FEES	TOTAL EXPENSE	PROFIT

NOTES

INVENTORY #			ITEM			BRAND	
DESCRIPTION							
SOURCE			LOCATION			COST	
CATEGORY	WOMEN ☐	MEN ☐	KIDS ☐	CONDITION	NEW WITH TAGS ☐	PREOWNED ☐	

DETAILS	MATERIAL	
	STYLE	
	FLAWS	

SIZING	TAG SIZE		WAIST		SHOULDER	
	CHEST		SLEEVE		INSEAM	
	LENGTH		NECK		RISE	

DATE SOLD	LISTING PRICE	SOLD PRICE	SHIPPING COST	SELLER FEES	TOTAL EXPENSE	PROFIT

NOTES

INVENTORY #			ITEM		BRAND	

DESCRIPTION	

SOURCE		LOCATION		COST	

CATEGORY	WOMEN ☐ MEN ☐ KIDS ☐	CONDITION	NEW WITH TAGS ☐ PREOWNED ☐

DETAILS	MATERIAL	
	STYLE	
	FLAWS	

SIZING	TAG SIZE		WAIST		SHOULDER	
	CHEST		SLEEVE		INSEAM	
	LENGTH		NECK		RISE	

DATE SOLD	LISTING PRICE	SOLD PRICE	SHIPPING COST	SELLER FEES	TOTAL EXPENSE	PROFIT

NOTES

INVENTORY #			ITEM		BRAND	

DESCRIPTION	

SOURCE		LOCATION		COST	

CATEGORY	WOMEN ☐ MEN ☐ KIDS ☐	CONDITION	NEW WITH TAGS ☐ PREOWNED ☐

DETAILS	MATERIAL	
	STYLE	
	FLAWS	

SIZING	TAG SIZE		WAIST		SHOULDER	
	CHEST		SLEEVE		INSEAM	
	LENGTH		NECK		RISE	

DATE SOLD	LISTING PRICE	SOLD PRICE	SHIPPING COST	SELLER FEES	TOTAL EXPENSE	PROFIT

NOTES

INVENTORY #		ITEM		BRAND	

DESCRIPTION	

SOURCE		LOCATION		COST	

CATEGORY	WOMEN ☐ MEN ☐ KIDS ☐	CONDITION	NEW WITH TAGS ☐ PREOWNED ☐

DETAILS	MATERIAL	
	STYLE	
	FLAWS	

SIZING	TAG SIZE		WAIST		SHOULDER	
	CHEST		SLEEVE		INSEAM	
	LENGTH		NECK		RISE	

DATE SOLD	LISTING PRICE	SOLD PRICE	SHIPPING COST	SELLER FEES	TOTAL EXPENSE	PROFIT

NOTES

INVENTORY #		ITEM		BRAND	

DESCRIPTION	

SOURCE		LOCATION		COST	

CATEGORY	WOMEN ☐ MEN ☐ KIDS ☐	CONDITION	NEW WITH TAGS ☐ PREOWNED ☐

DETAILS	MATERIAL	
	STYLE	
	FLAWS	

SIZING	TAG SIZE		WAIST		SHOULDER	
	CHEST		SLEEVE		INSEAM	
	LENGTH		NECK		RISE	

DATE SOLD	LISTING PRICE	SOLD PRICE	SHIPPING COST	SELLER FEES	TOTAL EXPENSE	PROFIT

NOTES

INVENTORY #			ITEM		BRAND	
DESCRIPTION						
SOURCE			LOCATION		COST	
CATEGORY	WOMEN ☐ MEN ☐ KIDS ☐		CONDITION	NEW WITH TAGS ☐	PREOWNED ☐	

DETAILS	MATERIAL	
	STYLE	
	FLAWS	

SIZING	TAG SIZE		WAIST		SHOULDER	
	CHEST		SLEEVE		INSEAM	
	LENGTH		NECK		RISE	

DATE SOLD	LISTING PRICE	SOLD PRICE	SHIPPING COST	SELLER FEES	TOTAL EXPENSE	PROFIT

NOTES

INVENTORY #			ITEM		BRAND	
DESCRIPTION						
SOURCE			LOCATION		COST	
CATEGORY	WOMEN ☐ MEN ☐ KIDS ☐		CONDITION	NEW WITH TAGS ☐	PREOWNED ☐	

DETAILS	MATERIAL	
	STYLE	
	FLAWS	

SIZING	TAG SIZE		WAIST		SHOULDER	
	CHEST		SLEEVE		INSEAM	
	LENGTH		NECK		RISE	

DATE SOLD	LISTING PRICE	SOLD PRICE	SHIPPING COST	SELLER FEES	TOTAL EXPENSE	PROFIT

NOTES

INVENTORY #		ITEM		BRAND	
DESCRIPTION					
SOURCE		LOCATION		COST	
CATEGORY	WOMEN ☐ MEN ☐ KIDS ☐	CONDITION	NEW WITH TAGS ☐	PREOWNED ☐	

DETAILS	MATERIAL	
	STYLE	
	FLAWS	

SIZING	TAG SIZE		WAIST		SHOULDER	
	CHEST		SLEEVE		INSEAM	
	LENGTH		NECK		RISE	

DATE SOLD	LISTING PRICE	SOLD PRICE	SHIPPING COST	SELLER FEES	TOTAL EXPENSE	PROFIT

NOTES

INVENTORY #		ITEM		BRAND	
DESCRIPTION					
SOURCE		LOCATION		COST	
CATEGORY	WOMEN ☐ MEN ☐ KIDS ☐	CONDITION	NEW WITH TAGS ☐	PREOWNED ☐	

DETAILS	MATERIAL	
	STYLE	
	FLAWS	

SIZING	TAG SIZE		WAIST		SHOULDER	
	CHEST		SLEEVE		INSEAM	
	LENGTH		NECK		RISE	

DATE SOLD	LISTING PRICE	SOLD PRICE	SHIPPING COST	SELLER FEES	TOTAL EXPENSE	PROFIT

NOTES

INVENTORY #			ITEM		BRAND	
DESCRIPTION						
SOURCE			LOCATION		COST	
CATEGORY	WOMEN ☐ MEN ☐ KIDS ☐		CONDITION	NEW WITH TAGS ☐	PREOWNED ☐	

DETAILS	MATERIAL	
	STYLE	
	FLAWS	

SIZING	TAG SIZE		WAIST		SHOULDER	
	CHEST		SLEEVE		INSEAM	
	LENGTH		NECK		RISE	

DATE SOLD	LISTING PRICE	SOLD PRICE	SHIPPING COST	SELLER FEES	TOTAL EXPENSE	PROFIT

NOTES

INVENTORY #			ITEM		BRAND	
DESCRIPTION						
SOURCE			LOCATION		COST	
CATEGORY	WOMEN ☐ MEN ☐ KIDS ☐		CONDITION	NEW WITH TAGS ☐	PREOWNED ☐	

DETAILS	MATERIAL	
	STYLE	
	FLAWS	

SIZING	TAG SIZE		WAIST		SHOULDER	
	CHEST		SLEEVE		INSEAM	
	LENGTH		NECK		RISE	

DATE SOLD	LISTING PRICE	SOLD PRICE	SHIPPING COST	SELLER FEES	TOTAL EXPENSE	PROFIT

NOTES

INVENTORY #		ITEM		BRAND	
DESCRIPTION					
SOURCE		LOCATION		COST	
CATEGORY	WOMEN ☐ MEN ☐ KIDS ☐	CONDITION	NEW WITH TAGS ☐	PREOWNED ☐	

DETAILS	MATERIAL	
	STYLE	
	FLAWS	

SIZING	TAG SIZE		WAIST		SHOULDER	
	CHEST		SLEEVE		INSEAM	
	LENGTH		NECK		RISE	

DATE SOLD	LISTING PRICE	SOLD PRICE	SHIPPING COST	SELLER FEES	TOTAL EXPENSE	PROFIT

NOTES

INVENTORY #		ITEM		BRAND	
DESCRIPTION					
SOURCE		LOCATION		COST	
CATEGORY	WOMEN ☐ MEN ☐ KIDS ☐	CONDITION	NEW WITH TAGS ☐	PREOWNED ☐	

DETAILS	MATERIAL	
	STYLE	
	FLAWS	

SIZING	TAG SIZE		WAIST		SHOULDER	
	CHEST		SLEEVE		INSEAM	
	LENGTH		NECK		RISE	

DATE SOLD	LISTING PRICE	SOLD PRICE	SHIPPING COST	SELLER FEES	TOTAL EXPENSE	PROFIT

NOTES

INVENTORY #		ITEM		BRAND	
DESCRIPTION					
SOURCE		LOCATION		COST	
CATEGORY	WOMEN ☐ MEN ☐ KIDS ☐	CONDITION	NEW WITH TAGS ☐	PREOWNED ☐	

DETAILS	MATERIAL	
	STYLE	
	FLAWS	

SIZING	TAG SIZE		WAIST		SHOULDER	
	CHEST		SLEEVE		INSEAM	
	LENGTH		NECK		RISE	

DATE SOLD	LISTING PRICE	SOLD PRICE	SHIPPING COST	SELLER FEES	TOTAL EXPENSE	PROFIT

NOTES

INVENTORY #		ITEM		BRAND	
DESCRIPTION					
SOURCE		LOCATION		COST	
CATEGORY	WOMEN ☐ MEN ☐ KIDS ☐	CONDITION	NEW WITH TAGS ☐	PREOWNED ☐	

DETAILS	MATERIAL	
	STYLE	
	FLAWS	

SIZING	TAG SIZE		WAIST		SHOULDER	
	CHEST		SLEEVE		INSEAM	
	LENGTH		NECK		RISE	

DATE SOLD	LISTING PRICE	SOLD PRICE	SHIPPING COST	SELLER FEES	TOTAL EXPENSE	PROFIT

NOTES

INVENTORY #		ITEM		BRAND	

DESCRIPTION	

SOURCE		LOCATION		COST	

CATEGORY	WOMEN ☐ MEN ☐ KIDS ☐	CONDITION	NEW WITH TAGS ☐ PREOWNED ☐

DETAILS	MATERIAL	
	STYLE	
	FLAWS	

SIZING	TAG SIZE		WAIST		SHOULDER	
	CHEST		SLEEVE		INSEAM	
	LENGTH		NECK		RISE	

DATE SOLD	LISTING PRICE	SOLD PRICE	SHIPPING COST	SELLER FEES	TOTAL EXPENSE	PROFIT

NOTES

INVENTORY #		ITEM		BRAND	

DESCRIPTION	

SOURCE		LOCATION		COST	

CATEGORY	WOMEN ☐ MEN ☐ KIDS ☐	CONDITION	NEW WITH TAGS ☐ PREOWNED ☐

DETAILS	MATERIAL	
	STYLE	
	FLAWS	

SIZING	TAG SIZE		WAIST		SHOULDER	
	CHEST		SLEEVE		INSEAM	
	LENGTH		NECK		RISE	

DATE SOLD	LISTING PRICE	SOLD PRICE	SHIPPING COST	SELLER FEES	TOTAL EXPENSE	PROFIT

NOTES

INVENTORY #			ITEM			BRAND	

DESCRIPTION	

SOURCE		LOCATION		COST	

CATEGORY	WOMEN ☐ MEN ☐ KIDS ☐	CONDITION	NEW WITH TAGS ☐ PREOWNED ☐

DETAILS	MATERIAL	
	STYLE	
	FLAWS	

SIZING	TAG SIZE		WAIST		SHOULDER	
	CHEST		SLEEVE		INSEAM	
	LENGTH		NECK		RISE	

DATE SOLD	LISTING PRICE	SOLD PRICE	SHIPPING COST	SELLER FEES	TOTAL EXPENSE	PROFIT

NOTES

INVENTORY #			ITEM			BRAND	

DESCRIPTION	

SOURCE		LOCATION		COST	

CATEGORY	WOMEN ☐ MEN ☐ KIDS ☐	CONDITION	NEW WITH TAGS ☐ PREOWNED ☐

DETAILS	MATERIAL	
	STYLE	
	FLAWS	

SIZING	TAG SIZE		WAIST		SHOULDER	
	CHEST		SLEEVE		INSEAM	
	LENGTH		NECK		RISE	

DATE SOLD	LISTING PRICE	SOLD PRICE	SHIPPING COST	SELLER FEES	TOTAL EXPENSE	PROFIT

NOTES

INVENTORY #		ITEM		BRAND	

DESCRIPTION	

SOURCE		LOCATION		COST	

CATEGORY	WOMEN ☐ MEN ☐ KIDS ☐	CONDITION	NEW WITH TAGS ☐ PREOWNED ☐

DETAILS	MATERIAL	
	STYLE	
	FLAWS	

SIZING	TAG SIZE		WAIST		SHOULDER	
	CHEST		SLEEVE		INSEAM	
	LENGTH		NECK		RISE	

DATE SOLD	LISTING PRICE	SOLD PRICE	SHIPPING COST	SELLER FEES	TOTAL EXPENSE	PROFIT

NOTES

INVENTORY #		ITEM		BRAND	

DESCRIPTION	

SOURCE		LOCATION		COST	

CATEGORY	WOMEN ☐ MEN ☐ KIDS ☐	CONDITION	NEW WITH TAGS ☐ PREOWNED ☐

DETAILS	MATERIAL	
	STYLE	
	FLAWS	

SIZING	TAG SIZE		WAIST		SHOULDER	
	CHEST		SLEEVE		INSEAM	
	LENGTH		NECK		RISE	

DATE SOLD	LISTING PRICE	SOLD PRICE	SHIPPING COST	SELLER FEES	TOTAL EXPENSE	PROFIT

NOTES

INVENTORY #		ITEM		BRAND	

DESCRIPTION	

SOURCE		LOCATION		COST	

CATEGORY	WOMEN ☐ MEN ☐ KIDS ☐	CONDITION	NEW WITH TAGS ☐ PREOWNED ☐

DETAILS	MATERIAL	
	STYLE	
	FLAWS	

SIZING	TAG SIZE		WAIST		SHOULDER	
	CHEST		SLEEVE		INSEAM	
	LENGTH		NECK		RISE	

DATE SOLD	LISTING PRICE	SOLD PRICE	SHIPPING COST	SELLER FEES	TOTAL EXPENSE	PROFIT

NOTES

INVENTORY #		ITEM		BRAND	

DESCRIPTION	

SOURCE		LOCATION		COST	

CATEGORY	WOMEN ☐ MEN ☐ KIDS ☐	CONDITION	NEW WITH TAGS ☐ PREOWNED ☐

DETAILS	MATERIAL	
	STYLE	
	FLAWS	

SIZING	TAG SIZE		WAIST		SHOULDER	
	CHEST		SLEEVE		INSEAM	
	LENGTH		NECK		RISE	

DATE SOLD	LISTING PRICE	SOLD PRICE	SHIPPING COST	SELLER FEES	TOTAL EXPENSE	PROFIT

NOTES

INVENTORY #			ITEM			BRAND	
DESCRIPTION							
SOURCE			LOCATION			COST	
CATEGORY	WOMEN ☐ MEN ☐ KIDS ☐		CONDITION	NEW WITH TAGS ☐		PREOWNED ☐	

DETAILS	MATERIAL	
	STYLE	
	FLAWS	

SIZING	TAG SIZE		WAIST		SHOULDER	
	CHEST		SLEEVE		INSEAM	
	LENGTH		NECK		RISE	

DATE SOLD	LISTING PRICE	SOLD PRICE	SHIPPING COST	SELLER FEES	TOTAL EXPENSE	PROFIT

NOTES

INVENTORY #			ITEM			BRAND	
DESCRIPTION							
SOURCE			LOCATION			COST	
CATEGORY	WOMEN ☐ MEN ☐ KIDS ☐		CONDITION	NEW WITH TAGS ☐		PREOWNED ☐	

DETAILS	MATERIAL	
	STYLE	
	FLAWS	

SIZING	TAG SIZE		WAIST		SHOULDER	
	CHEST		SLEEVE		INSEAM	
	LENGTH		NECK		RISE	

DATE SOLD	LISTING PRICE	SOLD PRICE	SHIPPING COST	SELLER FEES	TOTAL EXPENSE	PROFIT

NOTES

INVENTORY #		ITEM		BRAND	

DESCRIPTION	

SOURCE		LOCATION		COST	

CATEGORY	WOMEN ☐ MEN ☐ KIDS ☐	CONDITION	NEW WITH TAGS ☐ PREOWNED ☐

DETAILS	MATERIAL	
	STYLE	
	FLAWS	

SIZING	TAG SIZE		WAIST		SHOULDER	
	CHEST		SLEEVE		INSEAM	
	LENGTH		NECK		RISE	

DATE SOLD	LISTING PRICE	SOLD PRICE	SHIPPING COST	SELLER FEES	TOTAL EXPENSE	PROFIT

NOTES

INVENTORY #		ITEM		BRAND	

DESCRIPTION	

SOURCE		LOCATION		COST	

CATEGORY	WOMEN ☐ MEN ☐ KIDS ☐	CONDITION	NEW WITH TAGS ☐ PREOWNED ☐

DETAILS	MATERIAL	
	STYLE	
	FLAWS	

SIZING	TAG SIZE		WAIST		SHOULDER	
	CHEST		SLEEVE		INSEAM	
	LENGTH		NECK		RISE	

DATE SOLD	LISTING PRICE	SOLD PRICE	SHIPPING COST	SELLER FEES	TOTAL EXPENSE	PROFIT

NOTES

INVENTORY #			ITEM		BRAND	

DESCRIPTION	

SOURCE		LOCATION		COST	

CATEGORY	WOMEN ☐ MEN ☐ KIDS ☐	CONDITION	NEW WITH TAGS ☐ PREOWNED ☐

DETAILS	MATERIAL	
	STYLE	
	FLAWS	

SIZING	TAG SIZE		WAIST		SHOULDER	
	CHEST		SLEEVE		INSEAM	
	LENGTH		NECK		RISE	

DATE SOLD	LISTING PRICE	SOLD PRICE	SHIPPING COST	SELLER FEES	TOTAL EXPENSE	PROFIT

NOTES

INVENTORY #			ITEM		BRAND	

DESCRIPTION	

SOURCE		LOCATION		COST	

CATEGORY	WOMEN ☐ MEN ☐ KIDS ☐	CONDITION	NEW WITH TAGS ☐ PREOWNED ☐

DETAILS	MATERIAL	
	STYLE	
	FLAWS	

SIZING	TAG SIZE		WAIST		SHOULDER	
	CHEST		SLEEVE		INSEAM	
	LENGTH		NECK		RISE	

DATE SOLD	LISTING PRICE	SOLD PRICE	SHIPPING COST	SELLER FEES	TOTAL EXPENSE	PROFIT

NOTES

INVENTORY #			ITEM			BRAND		

DESCRIPTION	

SOURCE			LOCATION			COST	

CATEGORY	WOMEN ☐ MEN ☐ KIDS ☐	CONDITION	NEW WITH TAGS ☐ PREOWNED ☐

| DETAILS | MATERIAL | |
| | STYLE | |
	FLAWS	

| SIZING | TAG SIZE | | WAIST | | SHOULDER | |
| | CHEST | | SLEEVE | | INSEAM | |
	LENGTH		NECK		RISE	

DATE SOLD	LISTING PRICE	SOLD PRICE	SHIPPING COST	SELLER FEES	TOTAL EXPENSE	PROFIT

NOTES

INVENTORY #			ITEM			BRAND		

DESCRIPTION	

SOURCE			LOCATION			COST	

CATEGORY	WOMEN ☐ MEN ☐ KIDS ☐	CONDITION	NEW WITH TAGS ☐ PREOWNED ☐

| DETAILS | MATERIAL | |
| | STYLE | |
	FLAWS	

| SIZING | TAG SIZE | | WAIST | | SHOULDER | |
| | CHEST | | SLEEVE | | INSEAM | |
	LENGTH		NECK		RISE	

DATE SOLD	LISTING PRICE	SOLD PRICE	SHIPPING COST	SELLER FEES	TOTAL EXPENSE	PROFIT

NOTES

INVENTORY #		ITEM		BRAND	

DESCRIPTION	

SOURCE		LOCATION		COST	

CATEGORY WOMEN ☐ MEN ☐ KIDS ☐ CONDITION NEW WITH TAGS ☐ PREOWNED ☐

DETAILS	MATERIAL	
	STYLE	
	FLAWS	

SIZING	TAG SIZE		WAIST		SHOULDER	
	CHEST		SLEEVE		INSEAM	
	LENGTH		NECK		RISE	

DATE SOLD	LISTING PRICE	SOLD PRICE	SHIPPING COST	SELLER FEES	TOTAL EXPENSE	PROFIT

NOTES

INVENTORY #		ITEM		BRAND	

DESCRIPTION	

SOURCE		LOCATION		COST	

CATEGORY WOMEN ☐ MEN ☐ KIDS ☐ CONDITION NEW WITH TAGS ☐ PREOWNED ☐

DETAILS	MATERIAL	
	STYLE	
	FLAWS	

SIZING	TAG SIZE		WAIST		SHOULDER	
	CHEST		SLEEVE		INSEAM	
	LENGTH		NECK		RISE	

DATE SOLD	LISTING PRICE	SOLD PRICE	SHIPPING COST	SELLER FEES	TOTAL EXPENSE	PROFIT

NOTES

INVENTORY #		ITEM		BRAND	

DESCRIPTION	

SOURCE		LOCATION		COST	

CATEGORY	WOMEN ☐ MEN ☐ KIDS ☐	CONDITION	NEW WITH TAGS ☐ PREOWNED ☐

DETAILS	MATERIAL	
	STYLE	
	FLAWS	

SIZING	TAG SIZE		WAIST		SHOULDER	
	CHEST		SLEEVE		INSEAM	
	LENGTH		NECK		RISE	

DATE SOLD	LISTING PRICE	SOLD PRICE	SHIPPING COST	SELLER FEES	TOTAL EXPENSE	PROFIT

NOTES

INVENTORY #		ITEM		BRAND	

DESCRIPTION	

SOURCE		LOCATION		COST	

CATEGORY	WOMEN ☐ MEN ☐ KIDS ☐	CONDITION	NEW WITH TAGS ☐ PREOWNED ☐

DETAILS	MATERIAL	
	STYLE	
	FLAWS	

SIZING	TAG SIZE		WAIST		SHOULDER	
	CHEST		SLEEVE		INSEAM	
	LENGTH		NECK		RISE	

DATE SOLD	LISTING PRICE	SOLD PRICE	SHIPPING COST	SELLER FEES	TOTAL EXPENSE	PROFIT

NOTES

INVENTORY #			ITEM		BRAND	

DESCRIPTION	

SOURCE		LOCATION		COST	

CATEGORY	WOMEN ☐ MEN ☐ KIDS ☐	CONDITION	NEW WITH TAGS ☐ PREOWNED ☐

DETAILS	MATERIAL	
	STYLE	
	FLAWS	

SIZING	TAG SIZE		WAIST		SHOULDER	
	CHEST		SLEEVE		INSEAM	
	LENGTH		NECK		RISE	

DATE SOLD	LISTING PRICE	SOLD PRICE	SHIPPING COST	SELLER FEES	TOTAL EXPENSE	PROFIT

NOTES

INVENTORY #			ITEM		BRAND	

DESCRIPTION	

SOURCE		LOCATION		COST	

CATEGORY	WOMEN ☐ MEN ☐ KIDS ☐	CONDITION	NEW WITH TAGS ☐ PREOWNED ☐

DETAILS	MATERIAL	
	STYLE	
	FLAWS	

SIZING	TAG SIZE		WAIST		SHOULDER	
	CHEST		SLEEVE		INSEAM	
	LENGTH		NECK		RISE	

DATE SOLD	LISTING PRICE	SOLD PRICE	SHIPPING COST	SELLER FEES	TOTAL EXPENSE	PROFIT

NOTES

INVENTORY #			ITEM		BRAND	

DESCRIPTION	

SOURCE		LOCATION		COST	

CATEGORY	WOMEN ☐ MEN ☐ KIDS ☐	CONDITION	NEW WITH TAGS ☐ PREOWNED ☐

DETAILS	MATERIAL	
	STYLE	
	FLAWS	

SIZING	TAG SIZE		WAIST		SHOULDER	
	CHEST		SLEEVE		INSEAM	
	LENGTH		NECK		RISE	

DATE SOLD	LISTING PRICE	SOLD PRICE	SHIPPING COST	SELLER FEES	TOTAL EXPENSE	PROFIT

NOTES

INVENTORY #			ITEM		BRAND	

DESCRIPTION	

SOURCE		LOCATION		COST	

CATEGORY	WOMEN ☐ MEN ☐ KIDS ☐	CONDITION	NEW WITH TAGS ☐ PREOWNED ☐

DETAILS	MATERIAL	
	STYLE	
	FLAWS	

SIZING	TAG SIZE		WAIST		SHOULDER	
	CHEST		SLEEVE		INSEAM	
	LENGTH		NECK		RISE	

DATE SOLD	LISTING PRICE	SOLD PRICE	SHIPPING COST	SELLER FEES	TOTAL EXPENSE	PROFIT

NOTES

INVENTORY #			ITEM			BRAND	

DESCRIPTION	

SOURCE		LOCATION		COST	

CATEGORY	WOMEN ☐ MEN ☐ KIDS ☐	CONDITION	NEW WITH TAGS ☐	PREOWNED ☐

DETAILS	MATERIAL	
	STYLE	
	FLAWS	

SIZING	TAG SIZE		WAIST		SHOULDER	
	CHEST		SLEEVE		INSEAM	
	LENGTH		NECK		RISE	

DATE SOLD	LISTING PRICE	SOLD PRICE	SHIPPING COST	SELLER FEES	TOTAL EXPENSE	PROFIT

NOTES

INVENTORY #			ITEM			BRAND	

DESCRIPTION	

SOURCE		LOCATION		COST	

CATEGORY	WOMEN ☐ MEN ☐ KIDS ☐	CONDITION	NEW WITH TAGS ☐	PREOWNED ☐

DETAILS	MATERIAL	
	STYLE	
	FLAWS	

SIZING	TAG SIZE		WAIST		SHOULDER	
	CHEST		SLEEVE		INSEAM	
	LENGTH		NECK		RISE	

DATE SOLD	LISTING PRICE	SOLD PRICE	SHIPPING COST	SELLER FEES	TOTAL EXPENSE	PROFIT

NOTES

INVENTORY #			ITEM		BRAND	

DESCRIPTION

SOURCE			LOCATION		COST	

CATEGORY	WOMEN ☐ MEN ☐ KIDS ☐	CONDITION	NEW WITH TAGS ☐ PREOWNED ☐

DETAILS	MATERIAL	
	STYLE	
	FLAWS	

SIZING	TAG SIZE		WAIST		SHOULDER	
	CHEST		SLEEVE		INSEAM	
	LENGTH		NECK		RISE	

DATE SOLD	LISTING PRICE	SOLD PRICE	SHIPPING COST	SELLER FEES	TOTAL EXPENSE	PROFIT

NOTES

INVENTORY #			ITEM		BRAND	

DESCRIPTION

SOURCE			LOCATION		COST	

CATEGORY	WOMEN ☐ MEN ☐ KIDS ☐	CONDITION	NEW WITH TAGS ☐ PREOWNED ☐

DETAILS	MATERIAL	
	STYLE	
	FLAWS	

SIZING	TAG SIZE		WAIST		SHOULDER	
	CHEST		SLEEVE		INSEAM	
	LENGTH		NECK		RISE	

DATE SOLD	LISTING PRICE	SOLD PRICE	SHIPPING COST	SELLER FEES	TOTAL EXPENSE	PROFIT

NOTES

INVENTORY #		ITEM		BRAND	
DESCRIPTION					
SOURCE		LOCATION		COST	
CATEGORY	WOMEN ☐ MEN ☐ KIDS ☐	CONDITION	NEW WITH TAGS ☐	PREOWNED ☐	

DETAILS	MATERIAL	
	STYLE	
	FLAWS	

SIZING	TAG SIZE		WAIST		SHOULDER	
	CHEST		SLEEVE		INSEAM	
	LENGTH		NECK		RISE	

DATE SOLD	LISTING PRICE	SOLD PRICE	SHIPPING COST	SELLER FEES	TOTAL EXPENSE	PROFIT

NOTES

INVENTORY #		ITEM		BRAND	
DESCRIPTION					
SOURCE		LOCATION		COST	
CATEGORY	WOMEN ☐ MEN ☐ KIDS ☐	CONDITION	NEW WITH TAGS ☐	PREOWNED ☐	

DETAILS	MATERIAL	
	STYLE	
	FLAWS	

SIZING	TAG SIZE		WAIST		SHOULDER	
	CHEST		SLEEVE		INSEAM	
	LENGTH		NECK		RISE	

DATE SOLD	LISTING PRICE	SOLD PRICE	SHIPPING COST	SELLER FEES	TOTAL EXPENSE	PROFIT

NOTES

INVENTORY #		ITEM		BRAND	
DESCRIPTION					
SOURCE		LOCATION		COST	
CATEGORY	WOMEN ☐ MEN ☐ KIDS ☐	CONDITION	NEW WITH TAGS ☐	PREOWNED ☐	

DETAILS	MATERIAL	
	STYLE	
	FLAWS	

SIZING	TAG SIZE		WAIST		SHOULDER	
	CHEST		SLEEVE		INSEAM	
	LENGTH		NECK		RISE	

DATE SOLD	LISTING PRICE	SOLD PRICE	SHIPPING COST	SELLER FEES	TOTAL EXPENSE	PROFIT

NOTES

INVENTORY #		ITEM		BRAND	
DESCRIPTION					
SOURCE		LOCATION		COST	
CATEGORY	WOMEN ☐ MEN ☐ KIDS ☐	CONDITION	NEW WITH TAGS ☐	PREOWNED ☐	

DETAILS	MATERIAL	
	STYLE	
	FLAWS	

SIZING	TAG SIZE		WAIST		SHOULDER	
	CHEST		SLEEVE		INSEAM	
	LENGTH		NECK		RISE	

DATE SOLD	LISTING PRICE	SOLD PRICE	SHIPPING COST	SELLER FEES	TOTAL EXPENSE	PROFIT

NOTES

INVENTORY #		ITEM		BRAND	

DESCRIPTION	

SOURCE		LOCATION		COST	

CATEGORY	WOMEN ☐ MEN ☐ KIDS ☐	CONDITION	NEW WITH TAGS ☐ PREOWNED ☐

DETAILS	MATERIAL	
	STYLE	
	FLAWS	

SIZING	TAG SIZE		WAIST		SHOULDER	
	CHEST		SLEEVE		INSEAM	
	LENGTH		NECK		RISE	

DATE SOLD	LISTING PRICE	SOLD PRICE	SHIPPING COST	SELLER FEES	TOTAL EXPENSE	PROFIT

NOTES

INVENTORY #		ITEM		BRAND	

DESCRIPTION	

SOURCE		LOCATION		COST	

CATEGORY	WOMEN ☐ MEN ☐ KIDS ☐	CONDITION	NEW WITH TAGS ☐ PREOWNED ☐

DETAILS	MATERIAL	
	STYLE	
	FLAWS	

SIZING	TAG SIZE		WAIST		SHOULDER	
	CHEST		SLEEVE		INSEAM	
	LENGTH		NECK		RISE	

DATE SOLD	LISTING PRICE	SOLD PRICE	SHIPPING COST	SELLER FEES	TOTAL EXPENSE	PROFIT

NOTES

INVENTORY #		ITEM		BRAND	
DESCRIPTION					
SOURCE		LOCATION		COST	
CATEGORY	WOMEN ☐ MEN ☐ KIDS ☐	CONDITION	NEW WITH TAGS ☐	PREOWNED ☐	

DETAILS	MATERIAL	
	STYLE	
	FLAWS	

SIZING	TAG SIZE		WAIST		SHOULDER	
	CHEST		SLEEVE		INSEAM	
	LENGTH		NECK		RISE	

DATE SOLD	LISTING PRICE	SOLD PRICE	SHIPPING COST	SELLER FEES	TOTAL EXPENSE	PROFIT

NOTES

INVENTORY #		ITEM		BRAND	
DESCRIPTION					
SOURCE		LOCATION		COST	
CATEGORY	WOMEN ☐ MEN ☐ KIDS ☐	CONDITION	NEW WITH TAGS ☐	PREOWNED ☐	

DETAILS	MATERIAL	
	STYLE	
	FLAWS	

SIZING	TAG SIZE		WAIST		SHOULDER	
	CHEST		SLEEVE		INSEAM	
	LENGTH		NECK		RISE	

DATE SOLD	LISTING PRICE	SOLD PRICE	SHIPPING COST	SELLER FEES	TOTAL EXPENSE	PROFIT

NOTES

INVENTORY #		ITEM		BRAND	
DESCRIPTION					
SOURCE		LOCATION		COST	
CATEGORY	WOMEN ☐ MEN ☐ KIDS ☐	CONDITION	NEW WITH TAGS ☐	PREOWNED ☐	

DETAILS	MATERIAL	
	STYLE	
	FLAWS	

SIZING	TAG SIZE		WAIST		SHOULDER	
	CHEST		SLEEVE		INSEAM	
	LENGTH		NECK		RISE	

DATE SOLD	LISTING PRICE	SOLD PRICE	SHIPPING COST	SELLER FEES	TOTAL EXPENSE	PROFIT

NOTES

INVENTORY #		ITEM		BRAND	
DESCRIPTION					
SOURCE		LOCATION		COST	
CATEGORY	WOMEN ☐ MEN ☐ KIDS ☐	CONDITION	NEW WITH TAGS ☐	PREOWNED ☐	

DETAILS	MATERIAL	
	STYLE	
	FLAWS	

SIZING	TAG SIZE		WAIST		SHOULDER	
	CHEST		SLEEVE		INSEAM	
	LENGTH		NECK		RISE	

DATE SOLD	LISTING PRICE	SOLD PRICE	SHIPPING COST	SELLER FEES	TOTAL EXPENSE	PROFIT

NOTES

INVENTORY #			ITEM			BRAND	
DESCRIPTION							
SOURCE			LOCATION			COST	
CATEGORY	WOMEN ☐ MEN ☐ KIDS ☐		CONDITION	NEW WITH TAGS ☐		PREOWNED ☐	

DETAILS	MATERIAL	
	STYLE	
	FLAWS	

SIZING	TAG SIZE		WAIST		SHOULDER	
	CHEST		SLEEVE		INSEAM	
	LENGTH		NECK		RISE	

DATE SOLD	LISTING PRICE	SOLD PRICE	SHIPPING COST	SELLER FEES	TOTAL EXPENSE	PROFIT

NOTES

INVENTORY #			ITEM			BRAND	
DESCRIPTION							
SOURCE			LOCATION			COST	
CATEGORY	WOMEN ☐ MEN ☐ KIDS ☐		CONDITION	NEW WITH TAGS ☐		PREOWNED ☐	

DETAILS	MATERIAL	
	STYLE	
	FLAWS	

SIZING	TAG SIZE		WAIST		SHOULDER	
	CHEST		SLEEVE		INSEAM	
	LENGTH		NECK		RISE	

DATE SOLD	LISTING PRICE	SOLD PRICE	SHIPPING COST	SELLER FEES	TOTAL EXPENSE	PROFIT

NOTES

INVENTORY #		ITEM		BRAND	
DESCRIPTION					
SOURCE		LOCATION		COST	
CATEGORY	WOMEN ☐ MEN ☐ KIDS ☐	CONDITION	NEW WITH TAGS ☐	PREOWNED ☐	

DETAILS	MATERIAL	
	STYLE	
	FLAWS	

SIZING	TAG SIZE		WAIST		SHOULDER	
	CHEST		SLEEVE		INSEAM	
	LENGTH		NECK		RISE	

DATE SOLD	LISTING PRICE	SOLD PRICE	SHIPPING COST	SELLER FEES	TOTAL EXPENSE	PROFIT

NOTES

INVENTORY #		ITEM		BRAND	
DESCRIPTION					
SOURCE		LOCATION		COST	
CATEGORY	WOMEN ☐ MEN ☐ KIDS ☐	CONDITION	NEW WITH TAGS ☐	PREOWNED ☐	

DETAILS	MATERIAL	
	STYLE	
	FLAWS	

SIZING	TAG SIZE		WAIST		SHOULDER	
	CHEST		SLEEVE		INSEAM	
	LENGTH		NECK		RISE	

DATE SOLD	LISTING PRICE	SOLD PRICE	SHIPPING COST	SELLER FEES	TOTAL EXPENSE	PROFIT

NOTES

INVENTORY #		ITEM		BRAND	
DESCRIPTION					
SOURCE		LOCATION		COST	
CATEGORY	WOMEN ☐ MEN ☐ KIDS ☐	CONDITION	NEW WITH TAGS ☐	PREOWNED ☐	

DETAILS	MATERIAL	
	STYLE	
	FLAWS	

SIZING	TAG SIZE		WAIST		SHOULDER	
	CHEST		SLEEVE		INSEAM	
	LENGTH		NECK		RISE	

DATE SOLD	LISTING PRICE	SOLD PRICE	SHIPPING COST	SELLER FEES	TOTAL EXPENSE	PROFIT

NOTES

INVENTORY #		ITEM		BRAND	
DESCRIPTION					
SOURCE		LOCATION		COST	
CATEGORY	WOMEN ☐ MEN ☐ KIDS ☐	CONDITION	NEW WITH TAGS ☐	PREOWNED ☐	

DETAILS	MATERIAL	
	STYLE	
	FLAWS	

SIZING	TAG SIZE		WAIST		SHOULDER	
	CHEST		SLEEVE		INSEAM	
	LENGTH		NECK		RISE	

DATE SOLD	LISTING PRICE	SOLD PRICE	SHIPPING COST	SELLER FEES	TOTAL EXPENSE	PROFIT

NOTES

INVENTORY #		ITEM		BRAND	

DESCRIPTION	

SOURCE		LOCATION		COST	

CATEGORY	WOMEN ☐ MEN ☐ KIDS ☐	CONDITION	NEW WITH TAGS ☐ PREOWNED ☐

DETAILS	MATERIAL	
	STYLE	
	FLAWS	

SIZING	TAG SIZE		WAIST		SHOULDER	
	CHEST		SLEEVE		INSEAM	
	LENGTH		NECK		RISE	

DATE SOLD	LISTING PRICE	SOLD PRICE	SHIPPING COST	SELLER FEES	TOTAL EXPENSE	PROFIT

NOTES

INVENTORY #		ITEM		BRAND	

DESCRIPTION	

SOURCE		LOCATION		COST	

CATEGORY	WOMEN ☐ MEN ☐ KIDS ☐	CONDITION	NEW WITH TAGS ☐ PREOWNED ☐

DETAILS	MATERIAL	
	STYLE	
	FLAWS	

SIZING	TAG SIZE		WAIST		SHOULDER	
	CHEST		SLEEVE		INSEAM	
	LENGTH		NECK		RISE	

DATE SOLD	LISTING PRICE	SOLD PRICE	SHIPPING COST	SELLER FEES	TOTAL EXPENSE	PROFIT

NOTES

INVENTORY #		ITEM		BRAND	
DESCRIPTION					
SOURCE		LOCATION		COST	
CATEGORY	WOMEN ☐ MEN ☐ KIDS ☐	CONDITION	NEW WITH TAGS ☐	PREOWNED ☐	

DETAILS	MATERIAL	
	STYLE	
	FLAWS	

SIZING	TAG SIZE		WAIST		SHOULDER	
	CHEST		SLEEVE		INSEAM	
	LENGTH		NECK		RISE	

DATE SOLD	LISTING PRICE	SOLD PRICE	SHIPPING COST	SELLER FEES	TOTAL EXPENSE	PROFIT

NOTES

INVENTORY #		ITEM		BRAND	
DESCRIPTION					
SOURCE		LOCATION		COST	
CATEGORY	WOMEN ☐ MEN ☐ KIDS ☐	CONDITION	NEW WITH TAGS ☐	PREOWNED ☐	

DETAILS	MATERIAL	
	STYLE	
	FLAWS	

SIZING	TAG SIZE		WAIST		SHOULDER	
	CHEST		SLEEVE		INSEAM	
	LENGTH		NECK		RISE	

DATE SOLD	LISTING PRICE	SOLD PRICE	SHIPPING COST	SELLER FEES	TOTAL EXPENSE	PROFIT

NOTES

INVENTORY #		ITEM		BRAND	

DESCRIPTION	

SOURCE		LOCATION		COST	

CATEGORY	WOMEN ☐ MEN ☐ KIDS ☐	CONDITION	NEW WITH TAGS ☐ PREOWNED ☐

DETAILS	MATERIAL	
	STYLE	
	FLAWS	

SIZING	TAG SIZE		WAIST		SHOULDER	
	CHEST		SLEEVE		INSEAM	
	LENGTH		NECK		RISE	

DATE SOLD	LISTING PRICE	SOLD PRICE	SHIPPING COST	SELLER FEES	TOTAL EXPENSE	PROFIT

NOTES

INVENTORY #		ITEM		BRAND	

DESCRIPTION	

SOURCE		LOCATION		COST	

CATEGORY	WOMEN ☐ MEN ☐ KIDS ☐	CONDITION	NEW WITH TAGS ☐ PREOWNED ☐

DETAILS	MATERIAL	
	STYLE	
	FLAWS	

SIZING	TAG SIZE		WAIST		SHOULDER	
	CHEST		SLEEVE		INSEAM	
	LENGTH		NECK		RISE	

DATE SOLD	LISTING PRICE	SOLD PRICE	SHIPPING COST	SELLER FEES	TOTAL EXPENSE	PROFIT

NOTES

INVENTORY #		ITEM		BRAND	

DESCRIPTION	

SOURCE		LOCATION		COST	

CATEGORY	WOMEN ☐ MEN ☐ KIDS ☐	CONDITION	NEW WITH TAGS ☐ PREOWNED ☐

DETAILS	MATERIAL	
	STYLE	
	FLAWS	

SIZING	TAG SIZE		WAIST		SHOULDER	
	CHEST		SLEEVE		INSEAM	
	LENGTH		NECK		RISE	

DATE SOLD	LISTING PRICE	SOLD PRICE	SHIPPING COST	SELLER FEES	TOTAL EXPENSE	PROFIT

NOTES

INVENTORY #		ITEM		BRAND	

DESCRIPTION	

SOURCE		LOCATION		COST	

CATEGORY	WOMEN ☐ MEN ☐ KIDS ☐	CONDITION	NEW WITH TAGS ☐ PREOWNED ☐

DETAILS	MATERIAL	
	STYLE	
	FLAWS	

SIZING	TAG SIZE		WAIST		SHOULDER	
	CHEST		SLEEVE		INSEAM	
	LENGTH		NECK		RISE	

DATE SOLD	LISTING PRICE	SOLD PRICE	SHIPPING COST	SELLER FEES	TOTAL EXPENSE	PROFIT

NOTES

INVENTORY #		ITEM		BRAND	
DESCRIPTION					

SOURCE		LOCATION		COST	

CATEGORY	WOMEN ☐ MEN ☐ KIDS ☐	CONDITION	NEW WITH TAGS ☐ PREOWNED ☐

DETAILS	MATERIAL	
	STYLE	
	FLAWS	

SIZING	TAG SIZE		WAIST		SHOULDER	
	CHEST		SLEEVE		INSEAM	
	LENGTH		NECK		RISE	

DATE SOLD	LISTING PRICE	SOLD PRICE	SHIPPING COST	SELLER FEES	TOTAL EXPENSE	PROFIT

NOTES

INVENTORY #		ITEM		BRAND	
DESCRIPTION					

SOURCE		LOCATION		COST	

CATEGORY	WOMEN ☐ MEN ☐ KIDS ☐	CONDITION	NEW WITH TAGS ☐ PREOWNED ☐

DETAILS	MATERIAL	
	STYLE	
	FLAWS	

SIZING	TAG SIZE		WAIST		SHOULDER	
	CHEST		SLEEVE		INSEAM	
	LENGTH		NECK		RISE	

DATE SOLD	LISTING PRICE	SOLD PRICE	SHIPPING COST	SELLER FEES	TOTAL EXPENSE	PROFIT

NOTES

INVENTORY #		ITEM		BRAND	

DESCRIPTION	

SOURCE		LOCATION		COST	

CATEGORY   WOMEN ☐   MEN ☐   KIDS ☐   **CONDITION**   NEW WITH TAGS ☐   PREOWNED ☐

DETAILS	MATERIAL	
	STYLE	
	FLAWS	

SIZING	TAG SIZE		WAIST		SHOULDER	
	CHEST		SLEEVE		INSEAM	
	LENGTH		NECK		RISE	

DATE SOLD	LISTING PRICE	SOLD PRICE	SHIPPING COST	SELLER FEES	TOTAL EXPENSE	PROFIT

NOTES

INVENTORY #		ITEM		BRAND	

DESCRIPTION	

SOURCE		LOCATION		COST	

CATEGORY   WOMEN ☐   MEN ☐   KIDS ☐   **CONDITION**   NEW WITH TAGS ☐   PREOWNED ☐

DETAILS	MATERIAL	
	STYLE	
	FLAWS	

SIZING	TAG SIZE		WAIST		SHOULDER	
	CHEST		SLEEVE		INSEAM	
	LENGTH		NECK		RISE	

DATE SOLD	LISTING PRICE	SOLD PRICE	SHIPPING COST	SELLER FEES	TOTAL EXPENSE	PROFIT

NOTES

INVENTORY #		ITEM		BRAND	
DESCRIPTION					
SOURCE		LOCATION		COST	
CATEGORY	WOMEN ☐ MEN ☐ KIDS ☐	CONDITION	NEW WITH TAGS ☐	PREOWNED ☐	

DETAILS	MATERIAL	
	STYLE	
	FLAWS	

SIZING	TAG SIZE		WAIST		SHOULDER	
	CHEST		SLEEVE		INSEAM	
	LENGTH		NECK		RISE	

DATE SOLD	LISTING PRICE	SOLD PRICE	SHIPPING COST	SELLER FEES	TOTAL EXPENSE	PROFIT

NOTES

INVENTORY #		ITEM		BRAND	
DESCRIPTION					
SOURCE		LOCATION		COST	
CATEGORY	WOMEN ☐ MEN ☐ KIDS ☐	CONDITION	NEW WITH TAGS ☐	PREOWNED ☐	

DETAILS	MATERIAL	
	STYLE	
	FLAWS	

SIZING	TAG SIZE		WAIST		SHOULDER	
	CHEST		SLEEVE		INSEAM	
	LENGTH		NECK		RISE	

DATE SOLD	LISTING PRICE	SOLD PRICE	SHIPPING COST	SELLER FEES	TOTAL EXPENSE	PROFIT

NOTES

INVENTORY #			ITEM		BRAND	

DESCRIPTION	

SOURCE		LOCATION		COST	

CATEGORY	WOMEN ☐ MEN ☐ KIDS ☐	CONDITION	NEW WITH TAGS ☐ PREOWNED ☐

DETAILS	MATERIAL	
	STYLE	
	FLAWS	

SIZING	TAG SIZE		WAIST		SHOULDER	
	CHEST		SLEEVE		INSEAM	
	LENGTH		NECK		RISE	

DATE SOLD	LISTING PRICE	SOLD PRICE	SHIPPING COST	SELLER FEES	TOTAL EXPENSE	PROFIT

NOTES

INVENTORY #			ITEM		BRAND	

DESCRIPTION	

SOURCE		LOCATION		COST	

CATEGORY	WOMEN ☐ MEN ☐ KIDS ☐	CONDITION	NEW WITH TAGS ☐ PREOWNED ☐

DETAILS	MATERIAL	
	STYLE	
	FLAWS	

SIZING	TAG SIZE		WAIST		SHOULDER	
	CHEST		SLEEVE		INSEAM	
	LENGTH		NECK		RISE	

DATE SOLD	LISTING PRICE	SOLD PRICE	SHIPPING COST	SELLER FEES	TOTAL EXPENSE	PROFIT

NOTES

INVENTORY #		ITEM		BRAND	

DESCRIPTION	

SOURCE		LOCATION		COST	

CATEGORY	WOMEN ☐ MEN ☐ KIDS ☐	CONDITION	NEW WITH TAGS ☐ PREOWNED ☐

DETAILS	MATERIAL	
	STYLE	
	FLAWS	

SIZING	TAG SIZE		WAIST		SHOULDER	
	CHEST		SLEEVE		INSEAM	
	LENGTH		NECK		RISE	

DATE SOLD	LISTING PRICE	SOLD PRICE	SHIPPING COST	SELLER FEES	TOTAL EXPENSE	PROFIT

NOTES

INVENTORY #		ITEM		BRAND	

DESCRIPTION	

SOURCE		LOCATION		COST	

CATEGORY	WOMEN ☐ MEN ☐ KIDS ☐	CONDITION	NEW WITH TAGS ☐ PREOWNED ☐

DETAILS	MATERIAL	
	STYLE	
	FLAWS	

SIZING	TAG SIZE		WAIST		SHOULDER	
	CHEST		SLEEVE		INSEAM	
	LENGTH		NECK		RISE	

DATE SOLD	LISTING PRICE	SOLD PRICE	SHIPPING COST	SELLER FEES	TOTAL EXPENSE	PROFIT

NOTES

INVENTORY #			ITEM		BRAND		

DESCRIPTION	

SOURCE		LOCATION			COST	

CATEGORY	WOMEN ☐ MEN ☐ KIDS ☐	CONDITION	NEW WITH TAGS ☐ PREOWNED ☐

DETAILS	MATERIAL	
	STYLE	
	FLAWS	

SIZING	TAG SIZE		WAIST		SHOULDER	
	CHEST		SLEEVE		INSEAM	
	LENGTH		NECK		RISE	

DATE SOLD	LISTING PRICE	SOLD PRICE	SHIPPING COST	SELLER FEES	TOTAL EXPENSE	PROFIT

NOTES

INVENTORY #			ITEM		BRAND		

DESCRIPTION	

SOURCE		LOCATION			COST	

CATEGORY	WOMEN ☐ MEN ☐ KIDS ☐	CONDITION	NEW WITH TAGS ☐ PREOWNED ☐

DETAILS	MATERIAL	
	STYLE	
	FLAWS	

SIZING	TAG SIZE		WAIST		SHOULDER	
	CHEST		SLEEVE		INSEAM	
	LENGTH		NECK		RISE	

DATE SOLD	LISTING PRICE	SOLD PRICE	SHIPPING COST	SELLER FEES	TOTAL EXPENSE	PROFIT

NOTES

INVENTORY #		ITEM		BRAND	
DESCRIPTION					

SOURCE		LOCATION		COST	

CATEGORY	WOMEN ☐ MEN ☐ KIDS ☐	CONDITION	NEW WITH TAGS ☐	PREOWNED ☐

DETAILS	MATERIAL	
	STYLE	
	FLAWS	

SIZING	TAG SIZE		WAIST		SHOULDER	
	CHEST		SLEEVE		INSEAM	
	LENGTH		NECK		RISE	

DATE SOLD	LISTING PRICE	SOLD PRICE	SHIPPING COST	SELLER FEES	TOTAL EXPENSE	PROFIT

NOTES

INVENTORY #		ITEM		BRAND	
DESCRIPTION					

SOURCE		LOCATION		COST	

CATEGORY	WOMEN ☐ MEN ☐ KIDS ☐	CONDITION	NEW WITH TAGS ☐	PREOWNED ☐

DETAILS	MATERIAL	
	STYLE	
	FLAWS	

SIZING	TAG SIZE		WAIST		SHOULDER	
	CHEST		SLEEVE		INSEAM	
	LENGTH		NECK		RISE	

DATE SOLD	LISTING PRICE	SOLD PRICE	SHIPPING COST	SELLER FEES	TOTAL EXPENSE	PROFIT

NOTES

INVENTORY #			ITEM		BRAND	

DESCRIPTION	

SOURCE		LOCATION		COST	

CATEGORY	WOMEN ☐ MEN ☐ KIDS ☐	CONDITION	NEW WITH TAGS ☐ PREOWNED ☐

DETAILS	MATERIAL	
	STYLE	
	FLAWS	

SIZING	TAG SIZE		WAIST		SHOULDER	
	CHEST		SLEEVE		INSEAM	
	LENGTH		NECK		RISE	

DATE SOLD	LISTING PRICE	SOLD PRICE	SHIPPING COST	SELLER FEES	TOTAL EXPENSE	PROFIT

NOTES

INVENTORY #			ITEM		BRAND	

DESCRIPTION	

SOURCE		LOCATION		COST	

CATEGORY	WOMEN ☐ MEN ☐ KIDS ☐	CONDITION	NEW WITH TAGS ☐ PREOWNED ☐

DETAILS	MATERIAL	
	STYLE	
	FLAWS	

SIZING	TAG SIZE		WAIST		SHOULDER	
	CHEST		SLEEVE		INSEAM	
	LENGTH		NECK		RISE	

DATE SOLD	LISTING PRICE	SOLD PRICE	SHIPPING COST	SELLER FEES	TOTAL EXPENSE	PROFIT

NOTES

INVENTORY #			ITEM		BRAND	
DESCRIPTION						
SOURCE			LOCATION			COST
CATEGORY	WOMEN ☐ MEN ☐ KIDS ☐			CONDITION	NEW WITH TAGS ☐ PREOWNED ☐	

DETAILS	MATERIAL	
	STYLE	
	FLAWS	

SIZING	TAG SIZE		WAIST		SHOULDER	
	CHEST		SLEEVE		INSEAM	
	LENGTH		NECK		RISE	

DATE SOLD	LISTING PRICE	SOLD PRICE	SHIPPING COST	SELLER FEES	TOTAL EXPENSE	PROFIT

NOTES

INVENTORY #			ITEM		BRAND	
DESCRIPTION						
SOURCE			LOCATION			COST
CATEGORY	WOMEN ☐ MEN ☐ KIDS ☐			CONDITION	NEW WITH TAGS ☐ PREOWNED ☐	

DETAILS	MATERIAL	
	STYLE	
	FLAWS	

SIZING	TAG SIZE		WAIST		SHOULDER	
	CHEST		SLEEVE		INSEAM	
	LENGTH		NECK		RISE	

DATE SOLD	LISTING PRICE	SOLD PRICE	SHIPPING COST	SELLER FEES	TOTAL EXPENSE	PROFIT

NOTES

INVENTORY #			ITEM			BRAND	

DESCRIPTION	

SOURCE			LOCATION			COST	

CATEGORY	WOMEN ☐	MEN ☐	KIDS ☐	CONDITION	NEW WITH TAGS ☐	PREOWNED ☐

DETAILS	MATERIAL	
	STYLE	
	FLAWS	

SIZING	TAG SIZE		WAIST		SHOULDER	
	CHEST		SLEEVE		INSEAM	
	LENGTH		NECK		RISE	

DATE SOLD	LISTING PRICE	SOLD PRICE	SHIPPING COST	SELLER FEES	TOTAL EXPENSE	PROFIT

NOTES

INVENTORY #			ITEM			BRAND	

DESCRIPTION	

SOURCE			LOCATION			COST	

CATEGORY	WOMEN ☐	MEN ☐	KIDS ☐	CONDITION	NEW WITH TAGS ☐	PREOWNED ☐

DETAILS	MATERIAL	
	STYLE	
	FLAWS	

SIZING	TAG SIZE		WAIST		SHOULDER	
	CHEST		SLEEVE		INSEAM	
	LENGTH		NECK		RISE	

DATE SOLD	LISTING PRICE	SOLD PRICE	SHIPPING COST	SELLER FEES	TOTAL EXPENSE	PROFIT

NOTES

INVENTORY #			ITEM		BRAND	

DESCRIPTION	

SOURCE		LOCATION		COST	

CATEGORY	WOMEN ☐ MEN ☐ KIDS ☐	CONDITION	NEW WITH TAGS ☐ PREOWNED ☐

DETAILS	MATERIAL	
	STYLE	
	FLAWS	

SIZING	TAG SIZE		WAIST		SHOULDER	
	CHEST		SLEEVE		INSEAM	
	LENGTH		NECK		RISE	

DATE SOLD	LISTING PRICE	SOLD PRICE	SHIPPING COST	SELLER FEES	TOTAL EXPENSE	PROFIT

NOTES

INVENTORY #			ITEM		BRAND	

DESCRIPTION	

SOURCE		LOCATION		COST	

CATEGORY	WOMEN ☐ MEN ☐ KIDS ☐	CONDITION	NEW WITH TAGS ☐ PREOWNED ☐

DETAILS	MATERIAL	
	STYLE	
	FLAWS	

SIZING	TAG SIZE		WAIST		SHOULDER	
	CHEST		SLEEVE		INSEAM	
	LENGTH		NECK		RISE	

DATE SOLD	LISTING PRICE	SOLD PRICE	SHIPPING COST	SELLER FEES	TOTAL EXPENSE	PROFIT

NOTES

INVENTORY #		ITEM		BRAND	

DESCRIPTION	

SOURCE		LOCATION		COST	

CATEGORY	WOMEN ☐ MEN ☐ KIDS ☐	CONDITION	NEW WITH TAGS ☐ PREOWNED ☐

DETAILS	MATERIAL	
	STYLE	
	FLAWS	

SIZING	TAG SIZE		WAIST		SHOULDER	
	CHEST		SLEEVE		INSEAM	
	LENGTH		NECK		RISE	

DATE SOLD	LISTING PRICE	SOLD PRICE	SHIPPING COST	SELLER FEES	TOTAL EXPENSE	PROFIT

NOTES

INVENTORY #		ITEM		BRAND	

DESCRIPTION	

SOURCE		LOCATION		COST	

CATEGORY	WOMEN ☐ MEN ☐ KIDS ☐	CONDITION	NEW WITH TAGS ☐ PREOWNED ☐

DETAILS	MATERIAL	
	STYLE	
	FLAWS	

SIZING	TAG SIZE		WAIST		SHOULDER	
	CHEST		SLEEVE		INSEAM	
	LENGTH		NECK		RISE	

DATE SOLD	LISTING PRICE	SOLD PRICE	SHIPPING COST	SELLER FEES	TOTAL EXPENSE	PROFIT

NOTES

INVENTORY #			ITEM		BRAND	
DESCRIPTION						
SOURCE			LOCATION		COST	
CATEGORY	WOMEN ☐	MEN ☐	KIDS ☐	CONDITION	NEW WITH TAGS ☐	PREOWNED ☐

DETAILS	MATERIAL	
	STYLE	
	FLAWS	

SIZING	TAG SIZE		WAIST		SHOULDER	
	CHEST		SLEEVE		INSEAM	
	LENGTH		NECK		RISE	

DATE SOLD	LISTING PRICE	SOLD PRICE	SHIPPING COST	SELLER FEES	TOTAL EXPENSE	PROFIT

NOTES

INVENTORY #			ITEM		BRAND	
DESCRIPTION						
SOURCE			LOCATION		COST	
CATEGORY	WOMEN ☐	MEN ☐	KIDS ☐	CONDITION	NEW WITH TAGS ☐	PREOWNED ☐

DETAILS	MATERIAL	
	STYLE	
	FLAWS	

SIZING	TAG SIZE		WAIST		SHOULDER	
	CHEST		SLEEVE		INSEAM	
	LENGTH		NECK		RISE	

DATE SOLD	LISTING PRICE	SOLD PRICE	SHIPPING COST	SELLER FEES	TOTAL EXPENSE	PROFIT

NOTES

INVENTORY #			ITEM		BRAND	
DESCRIPTION						
SOURCE			LOCATION		COST	
CATEGORY	WOMEN ☐ MEN ☐ KIDS ☐		CONDITION	NEW WITH TAGS ☐	PREOWNED ☐	

DETAILS	MATERIAL	
	STYLE	
	FLAWS	

SIZING	TAG SIZE		WAIST		SHOULDER	
	CHEST		SLEEVE		INSEAM	
	LENGTH		NECK		RISE	

DATE SOLD	LISTING PRICE	SOLD PRICE	SHIPPING COST	SELLER FEES	TOTAL EXPENSE	PROFIT

NOTES

INVENTORY #			ITEM		BRAND	
DESCRIPTION						
SOURCE			LOCATION		COST	
CATEGORY	WOMEN ☐ MEN ☐ KIDS ☐		CONDITION	NEW WITH TAGS ☐	PREOWNED ☐	

DETAILS	MATERIAL	
	STYLE	
	FLAWS	

SIZING	TAG SIZE		WAIST		SHOULDER	
	CHEST		SLEEVE		INSEAM	
	LENGTH		NECK		RISE	

DATE SOLD	LISTING PRICE	SOLD PRICE	SHIPPING COST	SELLER FEES	TOTAL EXPENSE	PROFIT

NOTES

INVENTORY #		ITEM		BRAND	
DESCRIPTION					
SOURCE		LOCATION		COST	
CATEGORY	WOMEN ☐ MEN ☐ KIDS ☐	CONDITION	NEW WITH TAGS ☐	PREOWNED ☐	

DETAILS	MATERIAL	
	STYLE	
	FLAWS	

SIZING	TAG SIZE		WAIST		SHOULDER	
	CHEST		SLEEVE		INSEAM	
	LENGTH		NECK		RISE	

DATE SOLD	LISTING PRICE	SOLD PRICE	SHIPPING COST	SELLER FEES	TOTAL EXPENSE	PROFIT

NOTES

INVENTORY #		ITEM		BRAND	
DESCRIPTION					
SOURCE		LOCATION		COST	
CATEGORY	WOMEN ☐ MEN ☐ KIDS ☐	CONDITION	NEW WITH TAGS ☐	PREOWNED ☐	

DETAILS	MATERIAL	
	STYLE	
	FLAWS	

SIZING	TAG SIZE		WAIST		SHOULDER	
	CHEST		SLEEVE		INSEAM	
	LENGTH		NECK		RISE	

DATE SOLD	LISTING PRICE	SOLD PRICE	SHIPPING COST	SELLER FEES	TOTAL EXPENSE	PROFIT

NOTES

INVENTORY #			ITEM			BRAND	

DESCRIPTION	

SOURCE		LOCATION		COST	

CATEGORY	WOMEN ☐ MEN ☐ KIDS ☐	CONDITION	NEW WITH TAGS ☐ PREOWNED ☐

DETAILS	MATERIAL	
	STYLE	
	FLAWS	

SIZING	TAG SIZE		WAIST		SHOULDER	
	CHEST		SLEEVE		INSEAM	
	LENGTH		NECK		RISE	

DATE SOLD	LISTING PRICE	SOLD PRICE	SHIPPING COST	SELLER FEES	TOTAL EXPENSE	PROFIT

NOTES

INVENTORY #			ITEM			BRAND	

DESCRIPTION	

SOURCE		LOCATION		COST	

CATEGORY	WOMEN ☐ MEN ☐ KIDS ☐	CONDITION	NEW WITH TAGS ☐ PREOWNED ☐

DETAILS	MATERIAL	
	STYLE	
	FLAWS	

SIZING	TAG SIZE		WAIST		SHOULDER	
	CHEST		SLEEVE		INSEAM	
	LENGTH		NECK		RISE	

DATE SOLD	LISTING PRICE	SOLD PRICE	SHIPPING COST	SELLER FEES	TOTAL EXPENSE	PROFIT

NOTES

INVENTORY #		ITEM		BRAND	

DESCRIPTION	

SOURCE		LOCATION		COST	

CATEGORY	WOMEN ☐ MEN ☐ KIDS ☐	CONDITION	NEW WITH TAGS ☐ PREOWNED ☐

DETAILS	MATERIAL	
	STYLE	
	FLAWS	

SIZING	TAG SIZE		WAIST		SHOULDER	
	CHEST		SLEEVE		INSEAM	
	LENGTH		NECK		RISE	

DATE SOLD	LISTING PRICE	SOLD PRICE	SHIPPING COST	SELLER FEES	TOTAL EXPENSE	PROFIT

NOTES

INVENTORY #		ITEM		BRAND	

DESCRIPTION	

SOURCE		LOCATION		COST	

CATEGORY	WOMEN ☐ MEN ☐ KIDS ☐	CONDITION	NEW WITH TAGS ☐ PREOWNED ☐

DETAILS	MATERIAL	
	STYLE	
	FLAWS	

SIZING	TAG SIZE		WAIST		SHOULDER	
	CHEST		SLEEVE		INSEAM	
	LENGTH		NECK		RISE	

DATE SOLD	LISTING PRICE	SOLD PRICE	SHIPPING COST	SELLER FEES	TOTAL EXPENSE	PROFIT

NOTES

INVENTORY #		ITEM		BRAND	
DESCRIPTION					
SOURCE		LOCATION		COST	
CATEGORY	WOMEN ☐ MEN ☐ KIDS ☐	CONDITION	NEW WITH TAGS ☐	PREOWNED ☐	

DETAILS	MATERIAL	
	STYLE	
	FLAWS	

SIZING	TAG SIZE		WAIST		SHOULDER	
	CHEST		SLEEVE		INSEAM	
	LENGTH		NECK		RISE	

DATE SOLD	LISTING PRICE	SOLD PRICE	SHIPPING COST	SELLER FEES	TOTAL EXPENSE	PROFIT

NOTES

INVENTORY #		ITEM		BRAND	
DESCRIPTION					
SOURCE		LOCATION		COST	
CATEGORY	WOMEN ☐ MEN ☐ KIDS ☐	CONDITION	NEW WITH TAGS ☐	PREOWNED ☐	

DETAILS	MATERIAL	
	STYLE	
	FLAWS	

SIZING	TAG SIZE		WAIST		SHOULDER	
	CHEST		SLEEVE		INSEAM	
	LENGTH		NECK		RISE	

DATE SOLD	LISTING PRICE	SOLD PRICE	SHIPPING COST	SELLER FEES	TOTAL EXPENSE	PROFIT

NOTES

INVENTORY #		ITEM		BRAND	
DESCRIPTION					
SOURCE		LOCATION		COST	
CATEGORY	WOMEN ☐ MEN ☐ KIDS ☐	CONDITION	NEW WITH TAGS ☐	PREOWNED ☐	

DETAILS	MATERIAL	
	STYLE	
	FLAWS	

SIZING	TAG SIZE		WAIST		SHOULDER	
	CHEST		SLEEVE		INSEAM	
	LENGTH		NECK		RISE	

DATE SOLD	LISTING PRICE	SOLD PRICE	SHIPPING COST	SELLER FEES	TOTAL EXPENSE	PROFIT

NOTES

INVENTORY #		ITEM		BRAND	
DESCRIPTION					
SOURCE		LOCATION		COST	
CATEGORY	WOMEN ☐ MEN ☐ KIDS ☐	CONDITION	NEW WITH TAGS ☐	PREOWNED ☐	

DETAILS	MATERIAL	
	STYLE	
	FLAWS	

SIZING	TAG SIZE		WAIST		SHOULDER	
	CHEST		SLEEVE		INSEAM	
	LENGTH		NECK		RISE	

DATE SOLD	LISTING PRICE	SOLD PRICE	SHIPPING COST	SELLER FEES	TOTAL EXPENSE	PROFIT

NOTES

INVENTORY #		ITEM		BRAND	

DESCRIPTION	

SOURCE		LOCATION		COST	

CATEGORY	WOMEN ☐ MEN ☐ KIDS ☐	CONDITION	NEW WITH TAGS ☐ PREOWNED ☐

DETAILS	MATERIAL	
	STYLE	
	FLAWS	

SIZING	TAG SIZE		WAIST		SHOULDER	
	CHEST		SLEEVE		INSEAM	
	LENGTH		NECK		RISE	

DATE SOLD	LISTING PRICE	SOLD PRICE	SHIPPING COST	SELLER FEES	TOTAL EXPENSE	PROFIT

NOTES

INVENTORY #		ITEM		BRAND	

DESCRIPTION	

SOURCE		LOCATION		COST	

CATEGORY	WOMEN ☐ MEN ☐ KIDS ☐	CONDITION	NEW WITH TAGS ☐ PREOWNED ☐

DETAILS	MATERIAL	
	STYLE	
	FLAWS	

SIZING	TAG SIZE		WAIST		SHOULDER	
	CHEST		SLEEVE		INSEAM	
	LENGTH		NECK		RISE	

DATE SOLD	LISTING PRICE	SOLD PRICE	SHIPPING COST	SELLER FEES	TOTAL EXPENSE	PROFIT

NOTES

INVENTORY #		ITEM		BRAND	
DESCRIPTION					
SOURCE		LOCATION		COST	
CATEGORY	WOMEN ☐ MEN ☐ KIDS ☐	CONDITION	NEW WITH TAGS ☐	PREOWNED ☐	

DETAILS	MATERIAL	
	STYLE	
	FLAWS	

SIZING	TAG SIZE		WAIST		SHOULDER	
	CHEST		SLEEVE		INSEAM	
	LENGTH		NECK		RISE	

DATE SOLD	LISTING PRICE	SOLD PRICE	SHIPPING COST	SELLER FEES	TOTAL EXPENSE	PROFIT

NOTES

INVENTORY #		ITEM		BRAND	
DESCRIPTION					
SOURCE		LOCATION		COST	
CATEGORY	WOMEN ☐ MEN ☐ KIDS ☐	CONDITION	NEW WITH TAGS ☐	PREOWNED ☐	

DETAILS	MATERIAL	
	STYLE	
	FLAWS	

SIZING	TAG SIZE		WAIST		SHOULDER	
	CHEST		SLEEVE		INSEAM	
	LENGTH		NECK		RISE	

DATE SOLD	LISTING PRICE	SOLD PRICE	SHIPPING COST	SELLER FEES	TOTAL EXPENSE	PROFIT

NOTES

INVENTORY #			ITEM		BRAND		
DESCRIPTION							
SOURCE			LOCATION			COST	
CATEGORY	WOMEN ☐ MEN ☐ KIDS ☐		CONDITION	NEW WITH TAGS ☐		PREOWNED ☐	

DETAILS	MATERIAL	
	STYLE	
	FLAWS	

SIZING	TAG SIZE		WAIST		SHOULDER	
	CHEST		SLEEVE		INSEAM	
	LENGTH		NECK		RISE	

DATE SOLD	LISTING PRICE	SOLD PRICE	SHIPPING COST	SELLER FEES	TOTAL EXPENSE	PROFIT

NOTES

INVENTORY #			ITEM		BRAND		
DESCRIPTION							
SOURCE			LOCATION			COST	
CATEGORY	WOMEN ☐ MEN ☐ KIDS ☐		CONDITION	NEW WITH TAGS ☐		PREOWNED ☐	

DETAILS	MATERIAL	
	STYLE	
	FLAWS	

SIZING	TAG SIZE		WAIST		SHOULDER	
	CHEST		SLEEVE		INSEAM	
	LENGTH		NECK		RISE	

DATE SOLD	LISTING PRICE	SOLD PRICE	SHIPPING COST	SELLER FEES	TOTAL EXPENSE	PROFIT

NOTES

INVENTORY #		ITEM		BRAND	
DESCRIPTION					
SOURCE		LOCATION		COST	
CATEGORY	WOMEN ☐ MEN ☐ KIDS ☐	CONDITION	NEW WITH TAGS ☐	PREOWNED ☐	

DETAILS	MATERIAL	
	STYLE	
	FLAWS	

SIZING	TAG SIZE		WAIST		SHOULDER	
	CHEST		SLEEVE		INSEAM	
	LENGTH		NECK		RISE	

DATE SOLD	LISTING PRICE	SOLD PRICE	SHIPPING COST	SELLER FEES	TOTAL EXPENSE	PROFIT

NOTES

INVENTORY #		ITEM		BRAND	
DESCRIPTION					
SOURCE		LOCATION		COST	
CATEGORY	WOMEN ☐ MEN ☐ KIDS ☐	CONDITION	NEW WITH TAGS ☐	PREOWNED ☐	

DETAILS	MATERIAL	
	STYLE	
	FLAWS	

SIZING	TAG SIZE		WAIST		SHOULDER	
	CHEST		SLEEVE		INSEAM	
	LENGTH		NECK		RISE	

DATE SOLD	LISTING PRICE	SOLD PRICE	SHIPPING COST	SELLER FEES	TOTAL EXPENSE	PROFIT

NOTES

INVENTORY #			ITEM		BRAND		

DESCRIPTION	

SOURCE		LOCATION		COST	

CATEGORY	WOMEN ☐ MEN ☐ KIDS ☐	CONDITION	NEW WITH TAGS ☐ PREOWNED ☐

DETAILS	MATERIAL	
	STYLE	
	FLAWS	

SIZING	TAG SIZE		WAIST		SHOULDER	
	CHEST		SLEEVE		INSEAM	
	LENGTH		NECK		RISE	

DATE SOLD	LISTING PRICE	SOLD PRICE	SHIPPING COST	SELLER FEES	TOTAL EXPENSE	PROFIT

NOTES

INVENTORY #			ITEM		BRAND		

DESCRIPTION	

SOURCE		LOCATION		COST	

CATEGORY	WOMEN ☐ MEN ☐ KIDS ☐	CONDITION	NEW WITH TAGS ☐ PREOWNED ☐

DETAILS	MATERIAL	
	STYLE	
	FLAWS	

SIZING	TAG SIZE		WAIST		SHOULDER	
	CHEST		SLEEVE		INSEAM	
	LENGTH		NECK		RISE	

DATE SOLD	LISTING PRICE	SOLD PRICE	SHIPPING COST	SELLER FEES	TOTAL EXPENSE	PROFIT

NOTES

INVENTORY #			ITEM		BRAND	

DESCRIPTION	

SOURCE		LOCATION		COST	

CATEGORY	WOMEN ☐ MEN ☐ KIDS ☐	CONDITION	NEW WITH TAGS ☐ PREOWNED ☐

DETAILS	MATERIAL	
	STYLE	
	FLAWS	

SIZING	TAG SIZE		WAIST		SHOULDER	
	CHEST		SLEEVE		INSEAM	
	LENGTH		NECK		RISE	

DATE SOLD	LISTING PRICE	SOLD PRICE	SHIPPING COST	SELLER FEES	TOTAL EXPENSE	PROFIT

NOTES

INVENTORY #			ITEM		BRAND	

DESCRIPTION	

SOURCE		LOCATION		COST	

CATEGORY	WOMEN ☐ MEN ☐ KIDS ☐	CONDITION	NEW WITH TAGS ☐ PREOWNED ☐

DETAILS	MATERIAL	
	STYLE	
	FLAWS	

SIZING	TAG SIZE		WAIST		SHOULDER	
	CHEST		SLEEVE		INSEAM	
	LENGTH		NECK		RISE	

DATE SOLD	LISTING PRICE	SOLD PRICE	SHIPPING COST	SELLER FEES	TOTAL EXPENSE	PROFIT

NOTES

INVENTORY #			ITEM		BRAND	

DESCRIPTION	

SOURCE		LOCATION		COST	

CATEGORY	WOMEN ☐ MEN ☐ KIDS ☐	CONDITION	NEW WITH TAGS ☐ PREOWNED ☐

DETAILS	MATERIAL	
	STYLE	
	FLAWS	

SIZING	TAG SIZE		WAIST		SHOULDER	
	CHEST		SLEEVE		INSEAM	
	LENGTH		NECK		RISE	

DATE SOLD	LISTING PRICE	SOLD PRICE	SHIPPING COST	SELLER FEES	TOTAL EXPENSE	PROFIT

NOTES

INVENTORY #			ITEM		BRAND	

DESCRIPTION	

SOURCE		LOCATION		COST	

CATEGORY	WOMEN ☐ MEN ☐ KIDS ☐	CONDITION	NEW WITH TAGS ☐ PREOWNED ☐

DETAILS	MATERIAL	
	STYLE	
	FLAWS	

SIZING	TAG SIZE		WAIST		SHOULDER	
	CHEST		SLEEVE		INSEAM	
	LENGTH		NECK		RISE	

DATE SOLD	LISTING PRICE	SOLD PRICE	SHIPPING COST	SELLER FEES	TOTAL EXPENSE	PROFIT

NOTES

INVENTORY #		ITEM		BRAND	

DESCRIPTION	

SOURCE		LOCATION		COST	

CATEGORY	WOMEN ☐ MEN ☐ KIDS ☐	CONDITION	NEW WITH TAGS ☐ PREOWNED ☐

DETAILS	MATERIAL	
	STYLE	
	FLAWS	

SIZING	TAG SIZE		WAIST		SHOULDER	
	CHEST		SLEEVE		INSEAM	
	LENGTH		NECK		RISE	

DATE SOLD	LISTING PRICE	SOLD PRICE	SHIPPING COST	SELLER FEES	TOTAL EXPENSE	PROFIT

NOTES

INVENTORY #		ITEM		BRAND	

DESCRIPTION	

SOURCE		LOCATION		COST	

CATEGORY	WOMEN ☐ MEN ☐ KIDS ☐	CONDITION	NEW WITH TAGS ☐ PREOWNED ☐

DETAILS	MATERIAL	
	STYLE	
	FLAWS	

SIZING	TAG SIZE		WAIST		SHOULDER	
	CHEST		SLEEVE		INSEAM	
	LENGTH		NECK		RISE	

DATE SOLD	LISTING PRICE	SOLD PRICE	SHIPPING COST	SELLER FEES	TOTAL EXPENSE	PROFIT

NOTES

INVENTORY #		ITEM		BRAND	

DESCRIPTION	

SOURCE		LOCATION		COST	

CATEGORY	WOMEN ☐ MEN ☐ KIDS ☐	CONDITION	NEW WITH TAGS ☐ PREOWNED ☐

DETAILS	MATERIAL	
	STYLE	
	FLAWS	

SIZING	TAG SIZE		WAIST		SHOULDER	
	CHEST		SLEEVE		INSEAM	
	LENGTH		NECK		RISE	

DATE SOLD	LISTING PRICE	SOLD PRICE	SHIPPING COST	SELLER FEES	TOTAL EXPENSE	PROFIT

NOTES

INVENTORY #		ITEM		BRAND	

DESCRIPTION	

SOURCE		LOCATION		COST	

CATEGORY	WOMEN ☐ MEN ☐ KIDS ☐	CONDITION	NEW WITH TAGS ☐ PREOWNED ☐

DETAILS	MATERIAL	
	STYLE	
	FLAWS	

SIZING	TAG SIZE		WAIST		SHOULDER	
	CHEST		SLEEVE		INSEAM	
	LENGTH		NECK		RISE	

DATE SOLD	LISTING PRICE	SOLD PRICE	SHIPPING COST	SELLER FEES	TOTAL EXPENSE	PROFIT

NOTES

INVENTORY #		ITEM		BRAND	
DESCRIPTION					
SOURCE		LOCATION		COST	
CATEGORY	WOMEN ☐ MEN ☐ KIDS ☐	CONDITION	NEW WITH TAGS ☐	PREOWNED ☐	

DETAILS	MATERIAL	
	STYLE	
	FLAWS	

SIZING	TAG SIZE		WAIST		SHOULDER	
	CHEST		SLEEVE		INSEAM	
	LENGTH		NECK		RISE	

DATE SOLD	LISTING PRICE	SOLD PRICE	SHIPPING COST	SELLER FEES	TOTAL EXPENSE	PROFIT

NOTES

INVENTORY #		ITEM		BRAND	
DESCRIPTION					
SOURCE		LOCATION		COST	
CATEGORY	WOMEN ☐ MEN ☐ KIDS ☐	CONDITION	NEW WITH TAGS ☐	PREOWNED ☐	

DETAILS	MATERIAL	
	STYLE	
	FLAWS	

SIZING	TAG SIZE		WAIST		SHOULDER	
	CHEST		SLEEVE		INSEAM	
	LENGTH		NECK		RISE	

DATE SOLD	LISTING PRICE	SOLD PRICE	SHIPPING COST	SELLER FEES	TOTAL EXPENSE	PROFIT

NOTES

INVENTORY #		ITEM		BRAND	
DESCRIPTION					
SOURCE		LOCATION		COST	
CATEGORY	WOMEN ☐ MEN ☐ KIDS ☐	CONDITION	NEW WITH TAGS ☐	PREOWNED ☐	

DETAILS	MATERIAL	
	STYLE	
	FLAWS	

SIZING	TAG SIZE		WAIST		SHOULDER	
	CHEST		SLEEVE		INSEAM	
	LENGTH		NECK		RISE	

DATE SOLD	LISTING PRICE	SOLD PRICE	SHIPPING COST	SELLER FEES	TOTAL EXPENSE	PROFIT

NOTES

INVENTORY #		ITEM		BRAND	
DESCRIPTION					
SOURCE		LOCATION		COST	
CATEGORY	WOMEN ☐ MEN ☐ KIDS ☐	CONDITION	NEW WITH TAGS ☐	PREOWNED ☐	

DETAILS	MATERIAL	
	STYLE	
	FLAWS	

SIZING	TAG SIZE		WAIST		SHOULDER	
	CHEST		SLEEVE		INSEAM	
	LENGTH		NECK		RISE	

DATE SOLD	LISTING PRICE	SOLD PRICE	SHIPPING COST	SELLER FEES	TOTAL EXPENSE	PROFIT

NOTES

INVENTORY #			ITEM		BRAND	

DESCRIPTION

SOURCE		LOCATION		COST	

CATEGORY	WOMEN ☐	MEN ☐	KIDS ☐	CONDITION	NEW WITH TAGS ☐	PREOWNED ☐

DETAILS	MATERIAL	
	STYLE	
	FLAWS	

SIZING	TAG SIZE		WAIST		SHOULDER	
	CHEST		SLEEVE		INSEAM	
	LENGTH		NECK		RISE	

DATE SOLD	LISTING PRICE	SOLD PRICE	SHIPPING COST	SELLER FEES	TOTAL EXPENSE	PROFIT

NOTES

INVENTORY #			ITEM		BRAND	

DESCRIPTION

SOURCE		LOCATION		COST	

CATEGORY	WOMEN ☐	MEN ☐	KIDS ☐	CONDITION	NEW WITH TAGS ☐	PREOWNED ☐

DETAILS	MATERIAL	
	STYLE	
	FLAWS	

SIZING	TAG SIZE		WAIST		SHOULDER	
	CHEST		SLEEVE		INSEAM	
	LENGTH		NECK		RISE	

DATE SOLD	LISTING PRICE	SOLD PRICE	SHIPPING COST	SELLER FEES	TOTAL EXPENSE	PROFIT

NOTES

INVENTORY #			ITEM		BRAND	

DESCRIPTION	

SOURCE		LOCATION		COST	

CATEGORY	WOMEN ☐ MEN ☐ KIDS ☐	CONDITION	NEW WITH TAGS ☐ PREOWNED ☐

DETAILS	MATERIAL	
	STYLE	
	FLAWS	

SIZING	TAG SIZE		WAIST		SHOULDER	
	CHEST		SLEEVE		INSEAM	
	LENGTH		NECK		RISE	

DATE SOLD	LISTING PRICE	SOLD PRICE	SHIPPING COST	SELLER FEES	TOTAL EXPENSE	PROFIT

NOTES

INVENTORY #			ITEM		BRAND	

DESCRIPTION	

SOURCE		LOCATION		COST	

CATEGORY	WOMEN ☐ MEN ☐ KIDS ☐	CONDITION	NEW WITH TAGS ☐ PREOWNED ☐

DETAILS	MATERIAL	
	STYLE	
	FLAWS	

SIZING	TAG SIZE		WAIST		SHOULDER	
	CHEST		SLEEVE		INSEAM	
	LENGTH		NECK		RISE	

DATE SOLD	LISTING PRICE	SOLD PRICE	SHIPPING COST	SELLER FEES	TOTAL EXPENSE	PROFIT

NOTES

INVENTORY #		ITEM		BRAND	

DESCRIPTION	

SOURCE		LOCATION		COST	

CATEGORY	WOMEN ☐	MEN ☐	KIDS ☐	CONDITION	NEW WITH TAGS ☐	PREOWNED ☐

DETAILS	MATERIAL	
	STYLE	
	FLAWS	

SIZING	TAG SIZE		WAIST		SHOULDER	
	CHEST		SLEEVE		INSEAM	
	LENGTH		NECK		RISE	

DATE SOLD	LISTING PRICE	SOLD PRICE	SHIPPING COST	SELLER FEES	TOTAL EXPENSE	PROFIT

NOTES

INVENTORY #		ITEM		BRAND	

DESCRIPTION	

SOURCE		LOCATION		COST	

CATEGORY	WOMEN ☐	MEN ☐	KIDS ☐	CONDITION	NEW WITH TAGS ☐	PREOWNED ☐

DETAILS	MATERIAL	
	STYLE	
	FLAWS	

SIZING	TAG SIZE		WAIST		SHOULDER	
	CHEST		SLEEVE		INSEAM	
	LENGTH		NECK		RISE	

DATE SOLD	LISTING PRICE	SOLD PRICE	SHIPPING COST	SELLER FEES	TOTAL EXPENSE	PROFIT

NOTES

INVENTORY #		ITEM		BRAND	
DESCRIPTION					
SOURCE		LOCATION		COST	
CATEGORY	WOMEN ☐ MEN ☐ KIDS ☐	CONDITION	NEW WITH TAGS ☐	PREOWNED ☐	

DETAILS	MATERIAL	
	STYLE	
	FLAWS	

SIZING	TAG SIZE		WAIST		SHOULDER	
	CHEST		SLEEVE		INSEAM	
	LENGTH		NECK		RISE	

DATE SOLD	LISTING PRICE	SOLD PRICE	SHIPPING COST	SELLER FEES	TOTAL EXPENSE	PROFIT

NOTES

INVENTORY #		ITEM		BRAND	
DESCRIPTION					
SOURCE		LOCATION		COST	
CATEGORY	WOMEN ☐ MEN ☐ KIDS ☐	CONDITION	NEW WITH TAGS ☐	PREOWNED ☐	

DETAILS	MATERIAL	
	STYLE	
	FLAWS	

SIZING	TAG SIZE		WAIST		SHOULDER	
	CHEST		SLEEVE		INSEAM	
	LENGTH		NECK		RISE	

DATE SOLD	LISTING PRICE	SOLD PRICE	SHIPPING COST	SELLER FEES	TOTAL EXPENSE	PROFIT

NOTES

INVENTORY #		ITEM		BRAND	
DESCRIPTION					
SOURCE		LOCATION		COST	
CATEGORY	WOMEN ☐ MEN ☐ KIDS ☐	CONDITION	NEW WITH TAGS ☐	PREOWNED ☐	

DETAILS	MATERIAL	
	STYLE	
	FLAWS	

SIZING	TAG SIZE		WAIST		SHOULDER	
	CHEST		SLEEVE		INSEAM	
	LENGTH		NECK		RISE	

DATE SOLD	LISTING PRICE	SOLD PRICE	SHIPPING COST	SELLER FEES	TOTAL EXPENSE	PROFIT

NOTES

INVENTORY #		ITEM		BRAND	
DESCRIPTION					
SOURCE		LOCATION		COST	
CATEGORY	WOMEN ☐ MEN ☐ KIDS ☐	CONDITION	NEW WITH TAGS ☐	PREOWNED ☐	

DETAILS	MATERIAL	
	STYLE	
	FLAWS	

SIZING	TAG SIZE		WAIST		SHOULDER	
	CHEST		SLEEVE		INSEAM	
	LENGTH		NECK		RISE	

DATE SOLD	LISTING PRICE	SOLD PRICE	SHIPPING COST	SELLER FEES	TOTAL EXPENSE	PROFIT

NOTES

INVENTORY #			ITEM		BRAND	
DESCRIPTION						
SOURCE			LOCATION		COST	
CATEGORY	WOMEN ☐ MEN ☐ KIDS ☐		CONDITION	NEW WITH TAGS ☐ PREOWNED ☐		

DETAILS	MATERIAL	
	STYLE	
	FLAWS	

SIZING	TAG SIZE		WAIST		SHOULDER	
	CHEST		SLEEVE		INSEAM	
	LENGTH		NECK		RISE	

DATE SOLD	LISTING PRICE	SOLD PRICE	SHIPPING COST	SELLER FEES	TOTAL EXPENSE	PROFIT

NOTES

INVENTORY #			ITEM		BRAND	
DESCRIPTION						
SOURCE			LOCATION		COST	
CATEGORY	WOMEN ☐ MEN ☐ KIDS ☐		CONDITION	NEW WITH TAGS ☐ PREOWNED ☐		

DETAILS	MATERIAL	
	STYLE	
	FLAWS	

SIZING	TAG SIZE		WAIST		SHOULDER	
	CHEST		SLEEVE		INSEAM	
	LENGTH		NECK		RISE	

DATE SOLD	LISTING PRICE	SOLD PRICE	SHIPPING COST	SELLER FEES	TOTAL EXPENSE	PROFIT

NOTES

INVENTORY #			ITEM		BRAND	

DESCRIPTION	

SOURCE		LOCATION		COST	

CATEGORY	WOMEN ☐ MEN ☐ KIDS ☐	CONDITION	NEW WITH TAGS ☐ PREOWNED ☐

DETAILS	MATERIAL	
	STYLE	
	FLAWS	

SIZING	TAG SIZE		WAIST		SHOULDER	
	CHEST		SLEEVE		INSEAM	
	LENGTH		NECK		RISE	

DATE SOLD	LISTING PRICE	SOLD PRICE	SHIPPING COST	SELLER FEES	TOTAL EXPENSE	PROFIT

NOTES

INVENTORY #			ITEM		BRAND	

DESCRIPTION	

SOURCE		LOCATION		COST	

CATEGORY	WOMEN ☐ MEN ☐ KIDS ☐	CONDITION	NEW WITH TAGS ☐ PREOWNED ☐

DETAILS	MATERIAL	
	STYLE	
	FLAWS	

SIZING	TAG SIZE		WAIST		SHOULDER	
	CHEST		SLEEVE		INSEAM	
	LENGTH		NECK		RISE	

DATE SOLD	LISTING PRICE	SOLD PRICE	SHIPPING COST	SELLER FEES	TOTAL EXPENSE	PROFIT

NOTES

INVENTORY #			ITEM			BRAND	
DESCRIPTION							
SOURCE			LOCATION			COST	
CATEGORY	WOMEN ☐ MEN ☐ KIDS ☐		CONDITION	NEW WITH TAGS ☐		PREOWNED ☐	

DETAILS	MATERIAL	
	STYLE	
	FLAWS	

SIZING	TAG SIZE		WAIST		SHOULDER	
	CHEST		SLEEVE		INSEAM	
	LENGTH		NECK		RISE	

DATE SOLD	LISTING PRICE	SOLD PRICE	SHIPPING COST	SELLER FEES	TOTAL EXPENSE	PROFIT

NOTES

INVENTORY #			ITEM			BRAND	
DESCRIPTION							
SOURCE			LOCATION			COST	
CATEGORY	WOMEN ☐ MEN ☐ KIDS ☐		CONDITION	NEW WITH TAGS ☐		PREOWNED ☐	

DETAILS	MATERIAL	
	STYLE	
	FLAWS	

SIZING	TAG SIZE		WAIST		SHOULDER	
	CHEST		SLEEVE		INSEAM	
	LENGTH		NECK		RISE	

DATE SOLD	LISTING PRICE	SOLD PRICE	SHIPPING COST	SELLER FEES	TOTAL EXPENSE	PROFIT

NOTES

INVENTORY #		ITEM		BRAND	
DESCRIPTION					
SOURCE		LOCATION		COST	
CATEGORY	WOMEN ☐ MEN ☐ KIDS ☐	CONDITION	NEW WITH TAGS ☐ PREOWNED ☐		

DETAILS	MATERIAL	
	STYLE	
	FLAWS	

SIZING	TAG SIZE		WAIST		SHOULDER	
	CHEST		SLEEVE		INSEAM	
	LENGTH		NECK		RISE	

DATE SOLD	LISTING PRICE	SOLD PRICE	SHIPPING COST	SELLER FEES	TOTAL EXPENSE	PROFIT

NOTES

INVENTORY #		ITEM		BRAND	
DESCRIPTION					
SOURCE		LOCATION		COST	
CATEGORY	WOMEN ☐ MEN ☐ KIDS ☐	CONDITION	NEW WITH TAGS ☐ PREOWNED ☐		

DETAILS	MATERIAL	
	STYLE	
	FLAWS	

SIZING	TAG SIZE		WAIST		SHOULDER	
	CHEST		SLEEVE		INSEAM	
	LENGTH		NECK		RISE	

DATE SOLD	LISTING PRICE	SOLD PRICE	SHIPPING COST	SELLER FEES	TOTAL EXPENSE	PROFIT

NOTES

INVENTORY #		ITEM		BRAND	
DESCRIPTION					
SOURCE		LOCATION		COST	
CATEGORY	WOMEN ☐ MEN ☐ KIDS ☐	CONDITION	NEW WITH TAGS ☐	PREOWNED ☐	

DETAILS	MATERIAL	
	STYLE	
	FLAWS	

SIZING	TAG SIZE		WAIST		SHOULDER	
	CHEST		SLEEVE		INSEAM	
	LENGTH		NECK		RISE	

DATE SOLD	LISTING PRICE	SOLD PRICE	SHIPPING COST	SELLER FEES	TOTAL EXPENSE	PROFIT

NOTES

INVENTORY #		ITEM		BRAND	
DESCRIPTION					
SOURCE		LOCATION		COST	
CATEGORY	WOMEN ☐ MEN ☐ KIDS ☐	CONDITION	NEW WITH TAGS ☐	PREOWNED ☐	

DETAILS	MATERIAL	
	STYLE	
	FLAWS	

SIZING	TAG SIZE		WAIST		SHOULDER	
	CHEST		SLEEVE		INSEAM	
	LENGTH		NECK		RISE	

DATE SOLD	LISTING PRICE	SOLD PRICE	SHIPPING COST	SELLER FEES	TOTAL EXPENSE	PROFIT

NOTES

INVENTORY #			ITEM		BRAND	

DESCRIPTION	

SOURCE		LOCATION		COST	

CATEGORY	WOMEN ☐ MEN ☐ KIDS ☐	CONDITION	NEW WITH TAGS ☐ PREOWNED ☐

DETAILS	MATERIAL	
	STYLE	
	FLAWS	

SIZING	TAG SIZE		WAIST		SHOULDER	
	CHEST		SLEEVE		INSEAM	
	LENGTH		NECK		RISE	

DATE SOLD	LISTING PRICE	SOLD PRICE	SHIPPING COST	SELLER FEES	TOTAL EXPENSE	PROFIT

NOTES

INVENTORY #			ITEM		BRAND	

DESCRIPTION	

SOURCE		LOCATION		COST	

CATEGORY	WOMEN ☐ MEN ☐ KIDS ☐	CONDITION	NEW WITH TAGS ☐ PREOWNED ☐

DETAILS	MATERIAL	
	STYLE	
	FLAWS	

SIZING	TAG SIZE		WAIST		SHOULDER	
	CHEST		SLEEVE		INSEAM	
	LENGTH		NECK		RISE	

DATE SOLD	LISTING PRICE	SOLD PRICE	SHIPPING COST	SELLER FEES	TOTAL EXPENSE	PROFIT

NOTES

INVENTORY #		ITEM		BRAND	
DESCRIPTION					
SOURCE		LOCATION		COST	
CATEGORY	WOMEN ☐ MEN ☐ KIDS ☐	CONDITION	NEW WITH TAGS ☐	PREOWNED ☐	

DETAILS	MATERIAL	
	STYLE	
	FLAWS	

SIZING	TAG SIZE		WAIST		SHOULDER	
	CHEST		SLEEVE		INSEAM	
	LENGTH		NECK		RISE	

DATE SOLD	LISTING PRICE	SOLD PRICE	SHIPPING COST	SELLER FEES	TOTAL EXPENSE	PROFIT

NOTES

INVENTORY #		ITEM		BRAND	
DESCRIPTION					
SOURCE		LOCATION		COST	
CATEGORY	WOMEN ☐ MEN ☐ KIDS ☐	CONDITION	NEW WITH TAGS ☐	PREOWNED ☐	

DETAILS	MATERIAL	
	STYLE	
	FLAWS	

SIZING	TAG SIZE		WAIST		SHOULDER	
	CHEST		SLEEVE		INSEAM	
	LENGTH		NECK		RISE	

DATE SOLD	LISTING PRICE	SOLD PRICE	SHIPPING COST	SELLER FEES	TOTAL EXPENSE	PROFIT

NOTES

INVENTORY #		ITEM		BRAND	

DESCRIPTION	

SOURCE		LOCATION		COST	

CATEGORY	WOMEN ☐ MEN ☐ KIDS ☐	CONDITION	NEW WITH TAGS ☐ PREOWNED ☐

DETAILS	MATERIAL	
	STYLE	
	FLAWS	

SIZING	TAG SIZE		WAIST		SHOULDER	
	CHEST		SLEEVE		INSEAM	
	LENGTH		NECK		RISE	

DATE SOLD	LISTING PRICE	SOLD PRICE	SHIPPING COST	SELLER FEES	TOTAL EXPENSE	PROFIT

NOTES

INVENTORY #		ITEM		BRAND	

DESCRIPTION	

SOURCE		LOCATION		COST	

CATEGORY	WOMEN ☐ MEN ☐ KIDS ☐	CONDITION	NEW WITH TAGS ☐ PREOWNED ☐

DETAILS	MATERIAL	
	STYLE	
	FLAWS	

SIZING	TAG SIZE		WAIST		SHOULDER	
	CHEST		SLEEVE		INSEAM	
	LENGTH		NECK		RISE	

DATE SOLD	LISTING PRICE	SOLD PRICE	SHIPPING COST	SELLER FEES	TOTAL EXPENSE	PROFIT

NOTES

INVENTORY #		ITEM		BRAND	
DESCRIPTION					
SOURCE		LOCATION		COST	
CATEGORY	WOMEN ☐ MEN ☐ KIDS ☐	CONDITION	NEW WITH TAGS ☐ PREOWNED ☐		

DETAILS	MATERIAL	
	STYLE	
	FLAWS	

SIZING	TAG SIZE		WAIST		SHOULDER	
	CHEST		SLEEVE		INSEAM	
	LENGTH		NECK		RISE	

DATE SOLD	LISTING PRICE	SOLD PRICE	SHIPPING COST	SELLER FEES	TOTAL EXPENSE	PROFIT

NOTES

INVENTORY #		ITEM		BRAND	
DESCRIPTION					
SOURCE		LOCATION		COST	
CATEGORY	WOMEN ☐ MEN ☐ KIDS ☐	CONDITION	NEW WITH TAGS ☐ PREOWNED ☐		

DETAILS	MATERIAL	
	STYLE	
	FLAWS	

SIZING	TAG SIZE		WAIST		SHOULDER	
	CHEST		SLEEVE		INSEAM	
	LENGTH		NECK		RISE	

DATE SOLD	LISTING PRICE	SOLD PRICE	SHIPPING COST	SELLER FEES	TOTAL EXPENSE	PROFIT

NOTES

INVENTORY #		ITEM		BRAND	
DESCRIPTION					
SOURCE		LOCATION		COST	
CATEGORY	WOMEN ☐ MEN ☐ KIDS ☐	CONDITION	NEW WITH TAGS ☐	PREOWNED ☐	

DETAILS	MATERIAL	
	STYLE	
	FLAWS	

SIZING	TAG SIZE		WAIST		SHOULDER	
	CHEST		SLEEVE		INSEAM	
	LENGTH		NECK		RISE	

DATE SOLD	LISTING PRICE	SOLD PRICE	SHIPPING COST	SELLER FEES	TOTAL EXPENSE	PROFIT

NOTES

INVENTORY #		ITEM		BRAND	
DESCRIPTION					
SOURCE		LOCATION		COST	
CATEGORY	WOMEN ☐ MEN ☐ KIDS ☐	CONDITION	NEW WITH TAGS ☐	PREOWNED ☐	

DETAILS	MATERIAL	
	STYLE	
	FLAWS	

SIZING	TAG SIZE		WAIST		SHOULDER	
	CHEST		SLEEVE		INSEAM	
	LENGTH		NECK		RISE	

DATE SOLD	LISTING PRICE	SOLD PRICE	SHIPPING COST	SELLER FEES	TOTAL EXPENSE	PROFIT

NOTES

www.ingramcontent.com/pod-product-compliance
Lightning Source LLC
Chambersburg PA
CBHW051757200326
41597CB00025B/4590